Manifest West

Serenity and Severity

Manifest West

Serenity and Severity

Western
Press Books

WESTERN PRESS BOOKS
GUNNISON, COLORADO

ISBN: 978-1-60732-591-8

Library of Congress Control Number: 2016936122
Published in the United States of America

Western Press Books
Gunnison, Colorado

Cover image: SHUTTERSTOCK.COM

"The Burn, Four Years After" by Rick Kempa was previously published in *Keeping the Quiet* by Rick Kempa (Bellowing Ark Press).

"Plowshares" by John Haggerty was previously published in *MacGuffin* (Schoolcraft College).

"Tracking" by Nathan Alling Long was previously published in *Glimmer Train* (Glimmer Train Press) and Mother Knows (Washington Square Press).

"The Luckiest Boy in the World" by William Cass was previously published in POPLORISH (Old Growth Northwest).

STAFF

EDITOR
Caleb Seeling

CONSULTING EDITOR
Mark Todd

ASSISTANT EDITORS
Sheena Feiler
Sapphire Heien

DESIGN & LAYOUT
Sonya Unrein

CONTENTS

THE STORM
OF CIVILIZATION

CONTRIBUTOR NOTES

Introduction

The stark dichotomy of serenity and severity permeates the everyday, commonplace for those of us living in the West. Each of us observes the beautiful contrast of severe peaks and sharp precipices over the smooth serenity of valley floors and meadows as we drive through the many ranges that our region houses. Those of us who hike, raft, ski, run, and otherwise enjoy ourselves in Mother Nature know all too well that any shift in temperature or condition can be equally dazzling and deadly. Our ranchers are equally aware of this paradox, for rain and heat can both cultivate or destroy crops, depending on which season they occupy.

Yes, the *nature of the West* is both serene and severe—but this nature is not only of the outdoor variety. Our independent way of living can save us or strand us; conversely, our dedication to family can provide a network of others whose needs and desires we not only feel obligated to consider, but live to fulfill. The nature around us, the nature of our lives, and each of our individual natures are intertwined.

This complex theme offers numerous possible approaches, yet some are so interrelated that they are best understood in the context of each other. We have arranged this issue's selections into three categories, each representing a different interplay between humans, animals, nature, and the Western way of life. In "Nature's Duplicitous Embrace," the ways in which nature holds us and shapes us, both through love and beauty, and pain and tragedy, are dissected. In contrast, "The Storm of Civilization" investigates ways in which civilization and humanity affect and abuse the environment around us, and how our acts against nature return and impact our lives. Finally, "Growth and Resurgence" journeys through humans coming of age within nature, their personal growth as a direct result of the serenity and severity surrounding them, and nature's growth in spite of humanity and itself.

How better to explore the myriad of ways in which Western life embodies the serenity-severity dichotomy than through the voices of Westerners and West-lovers from diverse walks of life? In this fifth issue of *Manifest West*, twenty-nine writers offer their perspectives on the serenity and severity of life in our region. Representing various experiences and career paths, our writers range from those whom we may expect to be intimately acquainted with this duality—forest rangers, photographers, geographers, and ranchers—to the philosophers, lawyers, librarians, and military members whose own experiences are critical to rounding out our understanding of the serenity and severity of the land we call home.

Their submissions graced us in the shapes of short fiction, creative nonfiction, poetry, and—for the first time—flash fiction. Given the complexity of this issue's focus, what can we expect *other* than a panoramic interpretation of the theme in a diversity of forms?

NATURE'S DUPLICITOUS EMBRACE

ABIGAIL VAN KIRK

To Colorado, and Her Fickle Nature

Keep me shaking,
keep me shivering,

caress me with tendrils
of apathetic cold,

and I will learn to love
your stark unstable seasons.

Frigidity balances fiery hearts
and perhaps that's why I'm drawn to You.

GAIL DENHAM

All Night Vigil . . . Waiting for Fire

We held hands, five of us, perched on porch steps.
We watched gray columns of smoke rise above
forests we loved—columns surrounded us on three
sides. We could hear distant flames crackle

as the fire gobbled trees, brush—news reported homes
lost. We held hands, prayed for the brave ones trudging
through that madness with shovels, hoes, and ditch diggers.
I couldn't imagine facing that inferno head on. "God keep them."

"Mom, do I have to leave my rabbits?" Frankie was subdued.
I could only nod. My mind sorted: some family photos
and important papers gathered, but my doll collection, Vic's
artwork left behind. Dog cages stood ready. What did we forget?

Our car was packed, so full we might not all fit. Slowly
the sky blossomed with a sunset glow we'd never forget—
oranges, purples, brilliant red, as if the flames had shot
to the clouds and deliberately colored our skies.

Grandma Bertie brought out sandwiches—thick ham
on her homemade bread, upside down cake with fresh
peaches, hot and steaming, cold sodas. "Don't want
to waste this fresh fruit. Eat! It'll cheer you. After,
let's play that guessing game you kids like."

We sat outside nearly all night, fetching blankets and pillows
against the cool; Rachel and Frankie with heads on our laps;
waiting, hoping, praying. Grandma's rocker kept a steady
rhythm. Sprinklers whipped, wetting the roof; water dripped.

Suddenly, peeking from between two smoke columns, a full moon appeared. There it was—strange, tinted red, but whole and beautiful. Like a promise from God that fire might not leap to consume our world this time. A promise that whatever happened, there was order in the heavens.

LANCE NIZAMI

Fourteens from Thirty

A textured sea of wrinkled white recedes beneath the aeroplane
Colorado, colored white: the first sub-zero snows of Colorado
And here we cruise at thirty thousand feet

It's warm inside the cabin, and we soon forget the chill dry air outside
The chill dry air extends down to the land
It's Colorado, dry in winter, dry enough to turn men's skin to parchment

Colorado, white-flake-covered autumn Colorado, I can see you
November's barely here and plains and mountains lost their contours to the snow
And deep within the mountain valleys, elk will huddle in the bush, invisible

The streams are frozen over; beavers, fat with bark, sleep silent in their lodges
Colorado, Colorado; chilled and silent, little but a mouse disturbs the quietness
And far below me, flakes begin to fall; they're gently smoothing all to white
in Colorado.

REBECCA ARONSON

Los Alamos Fire

The city held its breath.
That is, we in the city held our breath.

The dog-walkers tugged leashes to a slow stroll
while dogs panted for speed.

The neighbors with their cream skin and kewpie eyes
rolled toward one another in the morning light.

The woman with a once-dark braid
gave stern instructions to her damaged son.

We simmered together with sore lungs and waited.
The air became visible

and settled around us seared particles
of forests. As odor contains remnants

of its object, my head aches with crumbled monuments
and spoiled crops, with the charred bodies of deer and wood mice,

radioactive ash the burning ground releases.
No one has said a grave is not a grave

when the buried thing still lives.
No one says it's time to leave.

REBECCA ARONSON

The First Act

There's wildfire
sheering the mountain,

leaving a smear of ash for a coat, cindering
knots of trees and abandoned hides.

What's left is a scorched shell so brittle
seedlings will storm through the surface.

From down here it will seem a riot of green gems
has erupted, a sleek new skin

to mask the burning city
which hovers at the periphery of sleep

coveting breath. We choose our dangers.
This high desert, piñons torchy

among parched understory, electrical sky,
radioactive remnants simmering in red rock,
this gun with its invisible trigger.

REBECCA ARONSON

Home

I wake blind in a striped cell.
I wake from a hot, black sleep
to find the sun, a manhole cover,
stomped down tight. I move through a field
of dry stalks rustling a reedy cantata,
woodwind in hollow sands, the music
of shrew and ragweed.
I came here for a mountain.
I came here for a poet. I came here
for something I imagined about horses.
I fell into a snake hole that held me.
When the rains came I was released
as high tide releases driftwood from the shoreline.

Some come to the desert to plant gardens;
some come to bury the dead
in shallow ditches. Some to disappear,
to turn themselves into century plants,
biding time. I know a woman
who turned tarantula.
Her night face is a painted skull.
She climbs out of her cavern
into the dark cover of cicada song, into cloud cover,
or snow pack, from a hole the wind carved.
My house is the color of dried blood.
When it rains, the walk runs red
and I am always
hoping for rain.

SCOTT T. STARBUCK

Canyon

I wanted to fish here but there were cliffs,
thorns, wasps, underwater drops
where men drowned.

Two- and three-foot leaping chromers,
fresh from the sea,
year after year.

Pine scent filled my lungs,
and blood on rocks
was fishes' and mine.

Petroglyphs and cliff trails showed
men netted here
thousands of years.

I can say more
but to know
you must go

before changing glaciers
melt experiences like these
maybe forever.

RONALD PICKETT

The Desert Night

There, now, the Sun touches the horizon, finally.
But it will be hours until the glazing, searing heat begins to ease.
The heat that is stored in the rocks and the sand and the dust.
And yet, almost at once, the air eases, and quiets, and softens.

It is the time of swift change, and all of the hidden animals and reptiles and
   insects know it.
It seems that even the plants, the greasy leafed shrubs, and the aloes, and the
   cactus know it too.
There is the sense of a collective sigh, a sigh that seems like a small puff of breeze;
We have survived another day of blazing sun and desiccating wind.
This is our time before the onset of night. It is uniquely serene.

The night brings terrors of its own.
The scorpions and spiders and snakes begin to move about not long after
   the dark sets in.
There is a flurry of activity; the scurrying of small feet and claws and scaled
   bellies in the sand.
And the flying, stinging insects begin to whirr through the thickening air.
Thrusting, crashing into the limbs and rocks and falling to the ground.
There, they dash for a hiding place to wait out the echoes of their wing sounds.

Before long, the overheated air begins to cool.
It seems to overreach its stable point and grow suddenly chilled, but still very,
   very dry.
The stars pop out of the rising gloom much clearer and brighter than they are
   supposed to be.
Punching their way through the inky blackness and shimmering, shimmering.
Even the moonless night is bright enough to barely mark the outlines of the
   thorn bushes,
And the prickly pears and the organ pipes, the jumping cactus and the
   stately saguaros.

They say that it only blooms once every hundred years, the century plant.
But I don't believe that. No one has been here a hundred years to find out!
They say that it blooms only at night, the cereus, and I do believe that.
They are carefully illuminated by the soft filtered starlight.
But the soft and extraordinary flowers of the cactus seem out of place.
As if they were attached there by a lost and aimless itinerant florist.

EVAN MORGAN WILLIAMS

Anasazi

Artis had been camping in the mesas before. He knew how it was. You roamed the canyons for the perfect campsite, you scrambled up the red rock, you gathered armloads of juniper sticks from the mesas and brought them down to build a fire. With any luck, your girlfriend had found an Anasazi firepit at the base of the cliffs, and you camped where people had camped for thousands of years. At night, the two of you toasted your happiness with plastic cups of wine. You ate shepherd's pie that you had wrapped in foil and cooked in the coals. As the fire died, you and your girl kept warm by dancing to music on the transistor radio, the Durango station, until the batteries froze. You slept cold, you slept close, and you woke up god-damned happy. Fresh snow on the yucca, silence in the canyon, juniper scent from the ashes of the fire.

Artis said nothing when Bernice complained about the cold, the falling snow, the steepness of the trails. He said nothing when Bernice complained about his setup of gear on the camp table, the stove on the wrong side, the water bottles too far to reach. When Artis prodded the shepherd's pie out of the coals, and the blackened foil hissed with steam that smelled like coriander and sage, and Bernice said, "I'm not eating that," Artis said nothing. Their baby, who had begun the trip happy and cooing, began to cry. Bernice held the baby against her chest, her cloud of breath close and cowering, and said, "How dare you endanger my child with all this cold?"

My child? Their child.

Artis kicked snow into the fire and said, "Let's go home."

But the car would not budge from the heavy snow. Artis would have to walk for help. Twenty miles to the highway. Darkness was coming. The tire tracks were filled in. Did Artis know the way? He thought of the family who, last year, had driven into the mesas too far and had gotten stuck. The dad had gone for help. A helicopter found the mom and kids a few days later, tired, cold, and hungry. The dad never made it.

Artis packed the rucksack for the long walk. He was anxious to chase the last hopeful light of day. Then he remembered something. He said, "Listen, I think there's a cabin down in this canyon. I don't know for certain, but I'm pretty sure."

Bernice said, "And you know this how?"

"I think I remember it from a trip in college."

"Why didn't you tell me?" Bernice paced around the dead campfire. The baby slept against her chest. Snowflakes settled on the baby's wool cap.

"I wasn't sure before, but now I'm sure."

"We're up here freezing to death, and you—"

He did not say, "You're supposed to enjoy nature." He did not say, "You're supposed to be god-damned happy."

Artis said this: "Alice and I saw a cabin down there once." He added, "And please quiet down. You'll wake the baby."

"Oh. This is about Alice. That's why you wouldn't tell me. Did you fuck her in that cabin, Artie? Obviously you did. I can't believe you. I don't even want to go to that cabin now."

"I'm climbing down to that cabin."

"Artie, you're going out to the highway. You'll flag down a car."

"I'm going to that cabin. I'm going to radio for help to save my wife and child."

Artis tried to pump his arms and legs. During the day, his gear had become wet from the snow, and now it was frozen stiff. Snow pants. Parka. Boots. Mittens. Cap. A scarf Bernice had knitted for him out of alpaca wool.

Bernice continued to pace around the firepit. "Don't take anything off. That's what happens, so they say. You remember that family? The dad took off his clothes. They found his body by following a trail of discarded clothes."

"I think I'll keep my clothes on."

"You're sure there's a cabin? Don't leave me up here while you look for a cabin you vaguely recall fucking your ex-girlfriend in."

"I'm sure there's a cabin, with a generator and a radio."

"At first you didn't remember, then you weren't sure, and then you were quite sure, but now you're so precisely sure that you even remember a radio?"

"Yes."

"It's all coming back to you. Oh, Artie, yes, yes."

"You know, the Anasazi culture collapsed while they argued over petty stuff. With the last of their warmth, they argued. Whether to rinse out the wine from the plastic cups before they stacked them. Whether to place them here or there. On their camp table. In their hogan."

"Did you fuck her in the night? Did you fuck her in the morning?"

"They must have felt the blood and heat under their skin. Did they even have plastic cups in those days?"

Artis stepped close enough to smell his baby and feel the warmth. The snowflakes were melting on the baby's cap. Artis and Bernice were supposed to be happy. This was the mesas. He knew how it was.

He put on the rucksack. He said, "Don't sleep in the car. It's warmer in the tent. I can't explain why, but it's absolutely true. Nothing but the cold air under the car."

He left Bernice and the baby in the cold and snow, and he picked his steps down the steep wash into the canyon, the red rock, where bare juniper roots were the only handholds. Farther down, the juniper thinned and the rock was bare. In the most distant light, he did see a cabin's tin roof through the cottonwoods. He was sure of it. The cabin. There would be dancing. Blood and heat on his skin. He remembered! Every slippery step took him closer. He was climbing alone, quietly, remembering how it was.

Deeper into the canyon, he found aspen trees clinging to cracks in the rock. A shoulder of rock jutted out, capped with snow. The snow slid away as he stepped on it. Far above, he saw Bernice with the baby, peering over the edge. She didn't seem to see him. Artis climbed down the shoulder of rock, and he couldn't see her anymore. It was quiet. Don't fall, he told himself. He was working up a sweat. He took off the scarf and let it drop. Did Bernice see that?

It was a difficult trail into the canyon, if it qualified as a trail at all, and Artis knew he would never be able to climb back up to the mesa. He had better be right about this cabin. He thought of the old times, dancing with Alice to the transistor radio. That took away the cold and pain, but he forced himself to stop thinking of the old times, because he needed to feel pain to survive. So he thought about Bernice. He thought of his baby. He climbed down through the aspens, tripping on their roots. This wasn't a trail. It was running away.

The pitch of the canyon eased to jumbled rock. Artis climbed over rocks mounded with snow. Sweat and snow soaked his boots. The cold air made his face ache. His hands went numb. His breath froze around his mouth. Tears froze at the corners of his eyes.

Bernice had devised hand signals. Artis was supposed to stop now and then, keeping her posted as he worked down the canyon. Every move, keep her posted.

The hell he would.

Artis and Alice had danced in the cabin. What was the signal for dancing? He was dancing in the snow now. He looked at his footprints all around. He had taken off his coat for dancing. His cap and mittens too. The trail had flattened out. It was the bottom of the canyon, a bed of smooth rocks where the creek had run dry. The cliffs blocked the sun, and it was cold as hell. Snow on the yuccas. Perfect quiet. Grey light. Artis picked up his things and walked down the creek bed easy as a stroll.

Artis found the cabin on a high bank above the creek bed. The cabin was locked, but he found the key hidden under a shingle by the door, exactly where they had found it last time. They had laughed about it then. He laughed about it now.

The cabin consisted of a big room—for dancing, Artis told himself—and a bunkroom in back. For fucking. Enough wood for a few fires. Artis made a fire, but the smoke was slow to draw because of the cold, and the cabin filled with smoke. The stove groaned from the heat, then it began to draw the smoke. Artis went outside to start the generator, but the noise of the thing was too much, and he turned it off. They had turned it off ten years ago for the same reason. Artis and Alice dancing! To come back to the mesas and see the crisp starlight above the black of the canyon walls, and to dance—the memory hurtled back! Artis went inside. Clumsy boots scraped a tired floor.

He lay on a bunk in the back room and shut his eyes. In his mind he heard Bach. The radio had died, country music from Durango, and Alice had begun whistling Bach tunes as Artis held her, and spun her, and held her again. Bach wrote dances. She told him so. *Allemande. Gigue. Menuet. Sarabande. He remembered the words.* He wanted to tell Bernice. He wanted to say he longed for happiness, that they, too, could be this way. Bernice could come to the cabin. Their baby would stay warm by the fire. The dishes would be neatly put away. He would whistle the music, and they would dance. She would come to him, fly over the snow to him. He would wait for them. He who could as easily fly away.

* * *

Artis stood outside as the morning sun cracked the top of the canyon. He was cold and perfect and alone. His breath tinkled as it froze. He heard another noise and saw Bernice sloughing down the creek bed. She carried the baby on her back and she swung her arms wide as she fought for footing in the snow. She was slipping and sliding from going too fast. Her hot breath floated, then froze and fell from the air.

Bernice dragged up to Artis. She was panting. She swung the baby carrier off her back. Her sweat had frozen into her hair. Artis was glad they were still alive. He was glad they had come. He didn't say anything. He took the baby.

Bernice said, "You threw away the scarf. I saw you."

He said, "It fell."

She said, "Why didn't you signal us?"

He said, "I did signal you. I made a fire. I wanted you here. God damn you, I wanted you here. Why would I want anyone else? Or anything else. Does it matter? You came. You wouldn't have come if I hadn't made the fire."

Bernice was still panting. She said, "Do you know how much work that was? Carrying the baby. We could have been killed."

"Yes."

"Well, you didn't say anything about it. You could have met me where the trail came down to the creek."

"You know, the Anasazi used to—"

"This where you fucked her, Artie?"

"Does it matter?"

"We froze in that car, you know."

"I told you not to sleep in the car."

Artis went in. He set the baby on a bottom bunk, wrapped in everything he could find, and he stoked the fire. He went out to start the generator while

Bernice tinkered with the CB radio. Artie came back in, but only because it was preferable to the racket of the generator outside. Bernice was talking on the radio. Artis didn't say anything. He wanted to say this: joy required too much effort to imagine. He took his baby from the bunk and sat by the woodstove and wept tears that did not freeze. His face felt hot. Tonight he would sleep with his memories. All the times they had sat on the bare rocks on top of the mesas and waited for the sunset, glad to wait forever, keeping each other warm—just memories now.

*   *   *

The snowmobiles came the next day. Park Service rangers: two crew-cut men and a young woman with her hair in a long thick braid. Artis asked them about Alice. Maybe they remembered her; she had worked as a summer ranger during college. They said they did not. It was late. They unloaded their packs and headed for the cabin.

Bernice was putting the cabin in order. Stock the wood bin, wipe down the kitchenette, sweep the porch. The baby slept on Bernice's back as she moved about the porch with a broom. The rangers said hello to Bernice, stomped the snow from their boots, and went inside. Bernice swept the snow away.

Bernice paused the sweeping and stared at the snowmobiles. "How are we all going to fit on those?"

"You just ride on the back and hold onto the driver, like on a motorcycle."

"What about the baby?"

"On your back, I suppose. Or on my back. I don't know."

"That's too dangerous."

"No, this, this, this, is too dangerous." Artis pointed to everything. The cabin, the canyon walls, the greying sky. If he could have pointed to cold, the god-damned cold, he would have pointed to it, but how did you point to something you felt all the way to your bones?

At night they danced to the rangers' transistor radio. Country music. Durango station. The rangers knew all the tunes. They had plenty of batteries! Bernice and the ranger woman took turns dancing with the ranger men. Bernice smiled and laughed. Artis held his warm, quiet baby and he watched

Bernice, and he watched the ranger woman, who had brushed out her long hair, and he didn't dance with anyone.

The rangers let Artis and Bernice have the bunkroom. For fucking. But Artis wouldn't fuck her. They could have fucked. They could have moved the baby out of the way, easy, and fucked. They didn't. Artis and Bernice each took a bunk, Bernice with the baby, Artis alone. He turned his back. He listened to the night. He felt his own warmth. He thought of everything at once, unmanageably, everything that could have been different. Smells and music and heat coming back. He thought of Alice.

From the other bunk, Bernice said, "I'm not going on those snowmobiles. I'm not putting my baby on one of those things."

"What choice do you have?"

"I'm not doing it."

Artis lay very still and thought about warmth. He said, "Can we please not talk? I'm trying to think."

"About all your poor little problems. Your only problem is to take care of us."

"That is the problem."

*   *   *

In the morning the rangers were sweeping the fresh snow off the snowmobiles. They were packing away their gear. It was going to be a bright, sunny day once the sun rose high enough to reach the canyon floor, but for now the canyon held only the grey light of shadows. The rangers were fiddling with the choke settings on their machines. The snowmobiles were bright yellow things.

Artis stepped from the cabin porch, walked over to the rangers, and said, "Go."

"What?"

"You heard me. Go. That means leave. Depart. Véte. Scram."

"You'll die out here."

"Go. Go the hell away."

The rangers looked at each other. They got on their snowmobiles and started up their angry noise.

The snowmobiles went off a ways. The last driver looked back. He said, "It's twenty fucking miles, pal." He said, "The funny thing is, you're not the first guy to be unhappy. We see this all the time. We know how it is." The snowmobiles went away, and the canyon was quiet. The canyon was cold.

Artis went inside to his life.

Bernice was seated by the woodstove. She was breastfeeding the baby. She said, "Artie, I don't—"

"Don't say anything. Good god, please don't say anything. Tidy up if you want something to do."

"Don't tell me what to do."

"Gladly."

She said, "You know what? We don't have a happily-ever-after. That's what you want, isn't it? That's what you think about, isn't it? Alice and you living happily ever after. Well, you and I don't have a happily-ever-after."

The baby began to cry. Bernice helped the baby find her tit. The baby latched on.

"Yes we do," Artis said. "We have this here right now. Completely and utterly for each other. Stuck with each other is more like it, but we don't have to see it that way."

Bernice said, "You know what? You don't regret the things you've done. You don't even regret the things you haven't done. You regret the things to come. The things with me."

Artis felt nothing and said, "I don't regret anything at all."

Night came. They cooked oatmeal, the last of their food, and sat by the fire. They drank warm water because they were out of tea. The cabin had enough juniper wood for maybe one more day.

Bernice said, "Artie, do you remember the stadium?"

"The stadium?"

"Mile High Stadium? The man at the Broncos game? The drunk man behind us who said something to me. You didn't fight him. You didn't fight for me. That little incident told me everything I needed know. I should have paid more attention."

"You would have found the fighting just as distasteful."

"That's not the point. I'm not Alice. You want Alice. You would have fought for Alice. I can't be your Alice." Bernice began to cry.

"The point is I'll fight for you now."

"But there's not anyone here."

"To call you a bitch? So I can kick his ass? We can get the snowmobilers back here . . ."

"You'd like that, wouldn't you? That was a lovely girl with the braid. One thing I don't understand, though. Artie, tell me this. Why didn't you stay with Alice?"

Artis didn't know. He and Alice had managed to secure no more happy-ever-after than anyone else. He didn't know. He only knew that by the end, they were fighting. He said, "She wanted coasters on the coffee table."

"Coasters are a good idea, Artie."

"The coffee table was boards and cinder blocks."

"So come on. What happened?"

"We came back. That's what happened. We got on with living."

Bernice stared at him. She didn't understand.

Artis got up from the fire.

Bernice said, "Wait. You left your glass."

Artis paused. He could pick up that god-damned glass. Or he could leave it on the floor. When you were dying in the cold, why did things have proper places anymore? He put it here, she put it there. This was their dance. Your certain way was not mine.

NATHAN ALLING LONG

Tracking

The train full of wedding guests struggled up into the mountains. What had appeared to the bride to be powdered sugar over a heap of cocoa in the distance was now distinct chunks of snow, dirty, gray, and hardened. Still, she beamed, listening to the murmurs then bursts of laughter throughout the train compartments. In the front car, three women, each holding a small bowl of rice, sat in a cluster. They took turns folding and refolding the lengths of their dresses, without thought, like cats rearranging their tails, while several men stood with glasses in hand, inventing progressively obscure toasts to celebrate the occasion.

The night before, an upright piano had been wheeled on board and a young man in a rented tux played voiceless renditions of songs everyone recognized but no one could name. It gave them all a great sense of familiarity and peace.

Everyone circulated through the train to the end car reserved for food as their palm-sized plates emptied. There, a man in white served meatballs, crab soufflé, and a cold vegetable stew. He was a student of biology taking on a summer job. Across from him a bar was set up, with champagne and ginger ale—*Only things bubbly*, the bride had said—with real glass glasses. Under the table a tiny broom and dust pan sat ready, in case a glass broke.

The women with the bowls of rice were all friends of the bride. One of them was pregnant and laughed at the whole affair. Another looked a little sad. The third seemed to have no expression at all. They were waiting for the photo session, with the Rockies as backdrop, to throw the contents of their bowls into the air. In the meantime, the expressionless one sifted the grains through a tiny hole where the tips of her fingers pressed together. The men saw an elk in the distance, mistook it for a caribou, and talked of hunting, though none of them had ever held a rifle in their lives.

The wedding had been in Boulder; this was only the reception train. Still, the men gathered with other men, the women with women, as though they were all in second grade, out on the playground. It was 2012, when divorces outnumbered weddings, and so weddings were really about the past, not the future, and those who came to them fell into old habits, as these men and women did, there on the train.

All, but one: an older woman who had nothing to do with either the groom or the bride. She had come to meet her daughter Judy at the end of the line, to bring her back to Boulder. Judy had been camping for a month, far in the mountains.

One of the wedding mothers—they seemed the same to those who weren't related, the same calm idiosyncratic politeness—went up to talk to Judy's mother.

"You're with the one they're picking up?" the wedding mother said. She was rubbing her fingers together in a circle, but beneath this anxiety rested a deep pool of calmness (her child was finally married, after all), which lay on an even deeper bed of anxiety (for how would it all turn out?).

"My daughter, yes," said Judy's mother. She thought of the wedding mother as a distraction; the wedding mother thought the same of her.

"Oh, heavens. How lovely," the wedding mother said, sipping from her glass. "Is she alone? Has it been long?"

Judy's mother hardly knew where to start. "Well, she does go out alone, quite often. She's a real outdoors type. But this time she's gone with Peter. They've been out there a month." She held back a smile of pride.

"A month! My!" the wedding mother said.

"Too long for a cell phone battery to last," Judy's mother said. "But we prearranged this day."

"Yes," said the other mother nodding. She glanced at the casual clothes Judy's mother wore and felt both sad and pleased by the formality of her own dress. She recovered from this thought and said, "At least she's with her husband."

"Oh no, just a boyfriend."

"But they're engaged?"

"No," said Judy's mother. There was a tiny silence between them. Then Judy's mother, against her will, said, "Not yet."

The mother of the bride—or groom—stood up, smiled. The train had been going quite slowly for a while, pushing its way up hill. The trip had been smooth. The wedding mother said, "I'm so glad you could join us. I hope you help yourself to champagne and to the buffet. There's so much food. We can't possibly eat it all, even with the whole trip back."

Judy's mother smiled in lieu of thank you, and the universal bond between mothers was resealed, like an envelope no one was ever to know had been broken.

A moment later, a piano string broke as it was struck, a loud slap of sound, which startled everyone. The best man took a red cocktail napkin—bunched and wet—and held it to his chest, pretending to be a caribou, shot.

"The altitude," the assistant engineer said, his jacket off, a heavy hand around one of the thin glasses. No one was certain if his comment was about the string or the man. He held his glass high to prevent it from spilling, though it looked as though if he were making a toast. "The altitude," he repeated and laughed.

The trip went on like this for an hour, until the horn sounded, which meant they were approaching the end of the track. Those who stuck their heads out the windows could see the end of the line: two round metal signs painted red, with a tiny supply shed off to the side, on the near edge of a snow-covered field.

Religiously, the train came to that spot every week. This afternoon, the shed door would be unlocked and the engineers would send a signal of their arrival. They would check supplies and replace the battery that powered the two-way radio. They would pick up Judy and her boyfriend. During all this, the wedding guests would walk around the snow field, which had once been a mining site, and take their wedding pictures against the sublimity of the mountains. Then, the engineers would fire up the engine on the other end of the train—there was no track for them to turn around—and return.

Except, of course, that Judy and her boyfriend were not there. Her mother and half a dozen wedding guests called out for them. They looked for messages posted on the outside of the shed. A couple of the wedding men who had brought jackets and boots traced the parameter of the field, looking for footprints and calling out the names again and again into the side of the mountain, "Judy! Peter! Judy!"

Judy's mother listened in terror, afraid that the sound of these strangers, men in tuxedos calling her daughter's name, would be the one memory she would carry from this day. *Let them appear*, she said, over and over, like a mantra. Twice she lost track of the men circling the field and when they reappeared, she momentarily mistook them for her daughter and Peter.

The engineers talked to her between tasks. "There's not been any major storm or nothing," the old one said.

It was August.

"They could have just gotten the days messed up," said the assistant. "It happens a lot with folks in the woods." The engineers were familiar with hikers who did not appear on schedule. In the past, such situations had ended in either way.

The bride and groom huddled close to each other and didn't leave the train. The man in white, the one who served the food, stayed at his post. He felt it was his duty. The piano player, however, took his break, eating quickly from a slightly chipped plate while he peered out the train window. Not all the wedding guests seemed to understand what was going on, and a few of them took several bottles of champagne and pitched them in the snow, like the world was their ice bucket. One held an ice pick he'd taken from the emergency box on the train, and with a bottle in the other hand, posed for the photographer.

It was late in the day, but the snow made flashes superfluous. The photographer was glad the gentle brush of his aperture as it shut was nearly silent. The sound, invisible to the mother missing her daughter, was a comfort to him, the register of a moment of time that he was living and recording. He believed he was an invisible figure in all his prints and reveled knowing his photographs would find themselves in strangers' houses, as though his very eyes would be there, even long after he and the people he photographed were gone.

They all waited until the last fabric of dusk slipped between the mountains.

"We're not supposed to, but we left the shed unlocked," the main engineer said to Judy's mother.

"There's food enough there for a week, but we'll get someone up here tomorrow, for sure," said the other. They were older men and knew what to say—but had little to say. They could not lie beyond the possibility of hope.

"Just five more minutes," Judy's mother begged.

But they had to return. The bride and groom had reservations at a ski lodge that night and many of the guests had to work the next day, though none of them mentioned these things—they simply offered silence as they boarded. The photographer closed his camera into its case as he passed Judy's mother.

The engine began to churn, like waves rapidly breaking on the shore. Everyone was in and the door was closed.

"Just five more minutes," Judy's mother said again to herself, but the train was already in motion. The mothers of the bride and groom then each took a turn comforting her, though it was impossible to know if they should be consoling or optimistic. And soon they realized that between them and Judy's mother lay the unspoken truth that she was missing a child and they were not, so they soon left for their own compartments.

The piano lid remained closed, its shiny surface reflecting the first stars of night. The rice bowls were stacked, the three women still. The pregnant one held her stomach in both hands, as though it were a porcelain bowl she might drop.

Judy's mother gazed out the window at the blue snow piled high against the tracks and at the wet slate color of the forest beyond. The man in white, the one who served the food, came up to her then and stroked her hand as the train rocked from the pressure of the brakes.

KAYE LYNNE BOOTH

Yucca! Yucca! Yucca!

They spatter the open mountain meadows
Like snow white spears reaching up
Above the tall grasses
Worshiping the sun.
Soft white flower spikes
Contrasting razor sharp spines.
The porcupines of the plant world.
Waiting, waiting for autumn winds
To dry their flower stalks into husks
That whisper the rattle of their name

SARAH FAWN MONTGOMERY

Pioneer

To lay down roots on the plains, try
to make something so untamed your own,
is to move closer, only a membrane of grass
separating you from the thrum that pumps beneath,
a tempting position what with
the horizon stretched before your gaze
like the back of a lover, naked and exposed.

But intimacy with this place is difficult,
the resistance of the flesh below
your weight, your work, your will.
Plow, pull from the earth your desire,
each season always the wild storms,
the slow build and danger, the release,
rush and sweet seeping after,
all moist and heaving green.

Trace the smooth thigh of the river,
your hand on the rounded belly of a hill—
suddenly the brittle bone, the spine
of the Rockies buckling and rising,
the dense weather that divide brings,
cackling lightning, rough winds,
the temperament towards destruction,
a permanent wilderness
despite all your best intentions.

SARAH FAWN MONTGOMERY

Altar

If Yosemite is a cathedral,
peaks like spires, highest point devotion
to a force worthy of the incline,
the mountain nave lengthening
to contain those who come to pray,
and the Grand Canyon is full of temples,
sacred spaces made in and of the rock,
worship for the strata of the place,
the depth of our impermanence,
then the Plains are an altar,
a flatness for sacrifice—
winters of isolation, of ice, of hunger,
the shimmer of mirage in the summer,
green skies sickly like premonition,
a funnel forming in the distance,
years bent at the plow for wheat, for corn,
body broken by the work of generations—
a great space on which to lay offerings—
a rock rubbed smooth by the bison
the feather of a barn swallow, cicada husk,
long grass gone crisp in the sun,
crabapples, chokecherries—
our compulsion to pray fed
by the vastness of sky and space
the smell of fragrant smoke,
fields afire for thousands of years,
blazing the way to rebirth.

THE STORM
OF CIVILIZATION

SARAH B. BOYLE

The Beast of the Plains

Sit down round our fire, I'll sing you a song
of the Beast who freezes time.
With a streak of white speed and one white eye
it stalks us rain and shine.
>> Whoop tie yay, ride away, ride away,
>> for the Beast brings death and decay.

The mountains cry trees when they hear it screech,
the snowolves howl and run.
The air turns cold as the ice on the plains,
and the world is as still as the sun.
>> Whoop tie yay, ride away, ride away,
>> for the Beast brings death and decay.

As black as powder and as lethal, too,
the Beast has guns not arms.
Snowolves once white now red with blood
lie dead in silent alarm.
>> Whoop tie yay, ride away, ride away,
>> for the Beast brings death and decay.

I carry my blade and Ad has her gun,
but we cannot kill the Beast.
So long as it roams and the sun burns cold
This land will know no peace.
>> Whoop tie yay, ride away, ride away,
>> for the Beast brings death and decay.

HEIDI E. BLANKENSHIP

Condor #122

Thunderbird, rain bird,
California Condor.
Shadow overhead,
wings longer than freedom,
they soar
like giants in the sky,
and yet
mistaken.
Twenty years of feathers
shot down
on the Kaibab Plateau,
leaving his mate alone
to raise a chick
at the Grand Canyon.
Twenty years spent scavenging;
twenty years
of dedicated volunteers,
of avian ecology,
downed in one shot
like the wolves who visit Utah,
each one mistaken for coyote.
Who could mistake a condor
for a turkey?
Before pulling the trigger,
could we think first?
Could we wait
and be absolutely certain?
Can we value every life?

BETSY BERNFELD

Sudden Storm

Sailing north on Jackson Lake
wing-and-wing, depth
250 feet, speed 1.7 knots, slow
peaceful pace without worry,
the dog stretched out on deck,
captain and mate lounging
in the catbird seats watching
the green water.

We pass through a patch
of debris—dirt, twigs, leaves,
flowers uprooted, water yellow
with pine pollen. Was it
evidence of last night's storm
that had sprinkled pine needles
across the marina? Or was it
a dirty remnant of the quarrel
at a campsite on the shore—

words flying like broken sticks,
sparks flaring from a log thrown
into the campfire, a disturbance
of soil where he knocked her down,
dragged her over the forest floor,
semen spraying uselessly, the dog
becoming agitated, shaking,
smelling blood, ready
to jump into the fray.

I hold tight to her collar
to keep her on board till we
pass again into clear placid

green like a white bird
emerging from the shadow
of a dark cloud.

DAVID LAVAR COY

Long Drive at Night through the Saguaro Forest

I tire of driving with only the visibility
of my headlights, the air conditioner on,
windows rolled up, watching the shadowy
figures of centurion cacti slip past,

following a road of beer cans, shredded tires,
mileage markers, urine jugs, empty hotels
and wind-destroyed trailers, wondering what
this place was like before the highway was cut.

I should stop, get out, take off my shirt, walk
through moonlight, be a pitiful old warrior,
though I have never fought for anything. I should
start my life over. I am one the young

would thrust a spear through as they enter
the citadel. There they would find decorated
clay pots, animal skins, baskets of maize,
a gold figurine on a floor smooth from kneelings.

They would think it a test. They would take
the figurine and destroy the rest, for it is
the job of the young to destroy
as it is the job of the old to remember.

What was I thinking of anyway?
Of fermented peyote in a gourd cup,
a circle of nearly-naked people telling
stories about how the world was created.

DAVID STALLINGS

Cold and Clear

This artesian spring
near Camp Mystery—
a snowmelt gift
of the vast upper basin.
Here, an underground flow
gurgles into sunlight,
welcomed by the magenta nod
of Jeffrey's shooting stars.

Year after year, we pause
to slake our thirst,
rub our feet, soak our bandanas,
then climb another mile
to the six-thousand-foot pass.
On our way down,
we fill bottles
for family and friends,
houseplants and altars,
grateful for these waters—
pure, dependable
even in late summer.

Until today—
another scorcher
in a year
of no snowpack.
This spring—
climate scientists
call it
a preview—
just dried mud
and rock.
         —Olympic Mountains, 2015

JUAN J. MORALES

Driving to Albuquerque

I've made this drive dozens of times,
but it's been years since I last
took the descent
into la frontera
between mountains and desert,
the city where I used to live.

I grow quiet for Raton Pass
with its charred trees stripped
of leaves, I stop in at my favorite
gas station in Romeroville
with fresh graffiti in the bathroom.

I sing till it hurts my throat to new and old
tunes
cranked and mess with the visor where I-25
curves just north of Santa Fe.

I cry for my selfish loss of love
with the Los Conchas Fire growing in the distance,
while a man I will never know
jumps off a bridge outside of Taos.

Approaching Albuquerque, I notice
that the Sandias, the mountains I never gave
enough credit, feel more
jagged
and lush. I pull over
to photograph when the sun
hits the range with the right glow
of October blood.

It is a few weeks before my thirty-first birthday
when I return to the Duke City,
to run back to another home away from,
where everyone locks dead bolts, no one drinks
from the tap, or leaves
their nice shit in the car, and it's all
an arid version of heaven
I didn't know I missed.

JOHN BRANTINGHAM

1850

Sean hears the man's horse clomping up from the foothills ten minutes before he sees him, so Sean hides Lena and children in the house, and he sits on the porch. It's a trapper. It's always trappers or miners unless it's people from the Potwisha tribe, and it would be all right if the stranger were a part of the tribe, but Sean's hidden Lena from white people all his married life.

Like Sean, the man is from Louisiana, but Baton Rouge, not New Orleans.

The man tells him that America made Zachary Taylor president.

"Really?"

"But he's already dead. A man named Millard Fillmore took over."

"Yeah," Sean says, and he wonders how long Lena can keep his baby boy silent.

"Also, they made California a state."

Sean cocks his head and thinks about that for a moment. "Why would they do that?"

The man laughs and shakes his head. "I don't know, but you're sitting in the United States of America."

Sean smiles because it's the smart move. Sean cheers because it's safe.

In an hour, the trapper moves on. In four hours, Sean and Lena have packed everything they will ever need to survive. In the afternoon, they are moving north and east, moving somewhere where there is no state or law. In a month they are living in the gentleness of the wild with neighbors who understand them: bears, wolves, buffalo.

TERRY SEVERHILL

ENVIRONMENT

The light raced towards the clouds, shattering,
Raining down shimmering rivulets of slivery gold incandescence
Over the distant mountains.
Ahh, such beauty, such promise.
False hope indeed.
Hundreds of kilometers into the vastness of utter desert.
What good knowing north from south?
East from west?
What direction salvation?
There has been no sign of life since Tobias fell dead
Two hours after noon, yesterday.
I could not bury him, no shovel, no strength.
Today I scan the horizon, the sky.
No sign of life, no lizards, snakes, no buzzards.
Nothing.
Odd, how this reminds me of the cube corral.
Its vastness, barren of life worth living.
Bereft of water cooler oasis, no sign of intelligent life.
No shelter from HR,
No respite from micro management.
  God save our souls.

JOHN HAGGERTY

Plowshares

Ted drove straight into the storm, didn't let up on the accelerator as the thunderheads built themselves up into great, black towers. The first drops hit the ground like bullets, but he didn't slow down, kept driving fast even when the rain came in thick, viscous sheets, turning the desert outside into a dark and rippling marine landscape. He drove through the washes and gullies, up over blasted limestone ridges, the rain briefly concealing the dead and desolate land, a place where nothing was soft, a place that looked like it had seen nothing but the back of God's hand.

He hated the desert, the endless, barren land, the tough herds of sheep among the creosote and greasewood, the narrow-eyed ranchers silent on their horses, barely moving as they watched him drive past—this was where the craziness was. No one sane would choose this life, this perverse embrace of suffering. It made him feel contaminated in some way, like the desert could creep into him, curl up inside, make him one of its own.

The rain slackened a bit, but the damage had already been done, swelling the arroyos with brown, arterial gouts of water. It was one of these that finally stopped him. The road had been pitching up and down for miles, over miniature ridges and down into ravines, cutting across the natural drainage of the desert. Coming up over a rise, he had to brake hard to stop the car from sliding into a cataract of violent, gritty water flooding across the road. He got out for a better look. The storm had ended, but the water still flowed, angry and dangerous. He turned around and kicked the fender of his car, putting a dent into the shiny white government paint of the brand-new '62 Plymouth.

Standing there, staring into the flooded ravine, he heard a noise behind him. Turning around, he saw a man on a horse. Typical rancher stock, dressed in a blue work shirt and jeans, stringy with work and deprivation.

"Looks like that ravine swelled up with all the rain," the rancher said.

"Yeah, didn't want to chance it in the car."

"That was smart. It would've taken you clean out to Saint George. Don't see many cars out on this road. Federal plates. Government man."

Ted moved toward him with an extended hand. "My name's Whitaker. Ted Whitaker." He mustered up the energy to give him his #2 smile, open and honest and friendly.

The rancher looked at him for a moment before shaking his hand. "Sam Wallace. What kind of government are you, Mr. Whitaker?"

He thought quickly. "It's, uh, Bureau of Land Management. BLM. I'm with the BLM."

"BLM." The rancher nodded slowly. "Don't get many BLM men looking like you. White shirt, tie. Nice clean car."

"Oh, you know, on my way to a meeting. Just got the car out of the pool. Give me a pickup truck and a pair of jeans any old day."

"Haven't seen you around. Usually we get Buster Thomas out here."

"Oh, yeah, old Buster. He's a character. But I'm not in this district. Just passing through. You know, on my way to Vegas. Meetings. Government work, you know, maybe get with some of the local color. Don't imagine you get out to Vegas much, but there's a lot to recommend it. Wine, women, song—that sort of thing. Especially the women part. Find some pretty showgirl to get close to . . ." He was talking too much, like he always did when he was uncomfortable. With an effort he closed his mouth into a #3 smile, boyish and conspiratorial.

The rancher watched him impassively for a moment. "Yeah, well, you're not getting there anytime soon." He nodded at the ravine. "Even when this water clears, the roadbed'll be washed out. They keep coming out and laying asphalt right across these washes, no culvert or nothing. Road washes out, they come back and lay more down. You'd think they'd know how to build a road in this day and age. Might be you can drive across it, might be not. But it'll be a while before we know for sure. You'd best come back to my place, have some dinner."

"Oh, I really couldn't trouble you. I'll just wait it out here . . ."

"Look, mister, odds are you're going to need some kind of help getting across there. I'm going back home to eat. It's just a half-mile back on the right. I reckon it'd be easier on all of us to come back here after we've gotten some food in us."

Ted weighed his options. He finally gave the rancher a nod. "I imagine a little bit of home cooking would do me some good. Been eating in too many of these sad-sack cafés. Life on the road, you know. Bachelor life. I envy a man who knows when to settle down." He forced his mouth shut and smiled at the rancher. "Half a mile back on the right." Sam rode off into the desert. Ted got back in his car and thought for a few minutes. Then he took out a Nevada map. There was a detour. It would add at least fifty miles, but he couldn't stand the idea of sitting in another rancher's house. Not before he got to Vegas, had some time to unwind, to get some space in between himself and the last couple of months.

He turned the car around and started accelerating back the way he had come. But in just a few seconds he had to slam on the brakes again. The rancher and his horse were standing in the middle of the road, blocking his way. As he came to a stop, the man motioned toward a dirt road on the right. Ted slumped his shoulders and then sat up straight and gave the man what he hoped to be a good approximation of his all-purpose smile. He started down the road, the rancher following him on horseback.

The house itself could have been on any one of the ranches he had seen in the last few years—bare gray wood, a few ramshackle outbuildings, all sun-faded and weather-beaten. But there were a few wrong notes—the clutter of tools not put away, weeds allowed to grow, maintenance deferred.

"Well, you certainly have yourself a beautiful place here, Mr. Wallace. Yessir. You sure have done wonders with this place. That's the old American pioneering spirit, you know. That's why I love this area—men who aren't afraid of a little hard work."

The rancher just nodded and said, "Why don't you come on in and meet the wife."

The house was neat inside, simple, bare furniture, some hand-tied rugs on the rough wood floor. It was hot, even with the coolness of rain blowing through. Sam motioned for him to sit at the dining room table and opened the door behind him. "Alma, come on out. We got company," he called into the next room.

The heat from the kitchen rolled over them as a thin, gray-haired woman hustled through. Dressed in prairie clothes made of rough cotton, she would have looked at home in a house just like this fifty years ago. She nodded formally to him.

"Ted, this is my wife, Alma." Sam turned to her. "Road's out again. Appears that Ted is some kind of government man."

The woman's skin had the slack look of someone who has recently lost weight. There was something behind her eyes that looked like a painful illness endured.

"Well, Alma, I sure am pleased to meet you." He gave her his lady-killer smile, boyish, friendly, but with a little edge. "Sam, I do believe that you have got just about the prettiest woman in Lincoln County hidden away out here. I am truly charmed, ma'am."

"Government," she said flatly. "What kind of government?"

"Uh, BLM," Ted replied. "BLM. Just traveling through. You know what they call us in some parts? The Bureau of Livestock and Mining. It's like they mean it as an insult. Personally, I'm proud of it. Helping out people like you. Real frontier types. Salt of the earth." He worked up a big smile and shone it around the room like a flashlight.

"Yeah. Well, we got a lot of atomic energy fellas out here for a while. You know, talking about the testing and all. You know any of them?"

"Well, I guess we cross paths now and again. Boy, that atomic stuff is something, isn't it? Harnessing the power of the atom." Another smile. "That's some stuff they're doing. Important work. Maybe the most important thing in the country right now." Ted looked at both of them, their hard gazes fixed on him. He searched his mind to see if he had ever met them before, but there had been so many meetings, so many introductions. His face felt stiff, like it had frozen into a dying parody of happiness.

Alma watched him for a while more and then said, "Well, I'll have dinner right out. Hope you like mutton, because that's about all we got anymore, these days."

As she turned back to the kitchen, Sam asked, "Will you be with us for the grace, Alma?"

She stopped for a moment and without turning around to face Sam, replied, "No, I don't reckon I have time for it today, Sam."

Sam drummed his fingers on the table, staring hard at the floor. He stayed silent while Ted prattled on about the weather, the roads, the Wallace ranch, his mouth seemingly beyond his control. Finally, Alma returned with two plates of food. After she went back into the kitchen, Sam bowed his head over his plate and muttered a benediction in a low, fast voice. "Dear Lord, bless this food and bless and keep this family and the guests in our home, and may we all be restored . . ." There was pause long enough that Ted looked up from his plate. Sam was motionless, his eyes downcast. Finally, he said, "In Jesus' name we pray," and looked up. As if waiting for the moment, Alma came back in with her own plate and sat down with them.

"So what kind of business brings you out to our country?" Alma asked, the question appearing not to want an answer at all.

"Oh, no business. Just passing through."

"Passing through."

"Yes, on my way to Vegas. I guess I would be there now if it weren't for that storm. One thing you have to say about these parts, the weather sure means business. It was like the wrath of God out there."

"The wrath of God? The wrath of God?" Sam's voice was tight and angry.

"Now, Sam," Alma said in a tired voice. "We don't need any of that right now."

"It just makes me wonder what he knows about the wrath of God, Mr. BLM over there."

Ted looked down at his plate, wondering again if he had met the two of them. This wasn't one of his counties, but anything was possible. His mind went back to the meetings. So many meetings. One every night for months. People, dozens at a time, men and women just like these two, crammed into sweltering schoolrooms and courthouses. He could smell their sweat, their dirt, the animals they tended. Ted's body poured with sweat too, and he would start to feel itchy and trapped. But Ted was professional. He had a job to do and he did it.

It was all about the delivery, he told people. It was a seduction, really, like trying to get a pretty woman in bed. He always started out slow and soft. Not like a scientist coming to bring the news to the backward natives, but like a neighbor, a friend.

"Hello, folks. I reckon you've been hearing a lot about what we're doing over at the Nevada Test Range by now. I'm here to tell you that everything you've heard—well, it's all true." He would scan the room, making eye contact with each person, giving them all a big, boyish, gee-whiz smile. "We're calling it Operation Plowshare. Harnessing the awesome power of the atom bomb for peace. We've got a new day dawning here, folks. A new day. Change is coming, big things brewing. We're all a big part of it. We're standing right next to the future here, standing right on the edge, and it's a bright day we're looking at, friends. A bright day indeed." He would begin articulating the wonders of the atomic age, things just around the corner. Free electricity. Food that cooks in seconds. Unbelievable marvels within reach, all due to the power of the atom.

He would look around, gauging the reaction. Most of the time it was a mixture of enthusiasm and bemusement—people sitting there open-mouthed, trying to understand, wanting to see the wonders he was describing.

"Oh, yes, it's a powerful trust we have been given. A stern covenant. We have been granted enormous power, and we have to learn to use it wisely." His voice, which had been open and enthusiastic, dropped to a low, confidential tone. "We have enemies. Everyone knows that. People who would do us harm, who would end our very way of life, who would enslave us." Again his voice would pick up. "And that's why we cannot rest, why we must continue on, why we must move forward. We here are at the vanguard. We are the men and women of the future. We are the ones who will carry this nation on toward its great, ordained destiny. A big part of this is the testing. We have to test our power. Make sure it's right. We're all part of the project. It's perfectly safe, perfectly natural, and crucial to our future. We're in the biggest darned science lab in the world. Heck, maybe the universe. And when we're done with our experiments, when we have completed our work, then we will have truly mastered nature. We will have mastered the most basic, most powerful forces of the universe. And all of us, every one of us, will be able to say that we were there at the beginning. We were there at the beginning, and when the door to the future appeared, we opened that door. Yes, my friends, we opened that door, and by golly, we walked on through."

Before his last, thunderous words finished, the simple men and women he was addressing would jump to their feet, their faces glowing with the pride of being the leaders, the guardians of the atomic age. He would beam right back at them, a full, glory-of-God #10. But inside he felt nothing but pity for these poor saps with their backward ways and their aw-shucks mannerisms. They were the past, but they didn't know it. When the new era dawned, every single one of them would be left behind. What use would there be for such people, these ranchers and farmers, dirty and hard and worn from the sheer, teeth-gritting effort of just staying alive in these godforsaken places? The future was going to roll right over them, and it would leave nothing behind. But he just smiled, smiled not at them, but through them, to the grand destiny that he was helping the country reach. But that was months ago, and things were different now. Now his job meant talking to people like Sam and Alma in farmhouses a lot like this one. It meant suspicious looks and confusion and barely concealed pain, and it had started to fill Ted with a deep and arid weariness.

"Is there something wrong with our food?" Sam's voice made him start, and he realized that he had been pushing his food around his plate without eating.

"Well, I guess . . . I just had a big lunch, I guess. Don't have much of an appetite. And I'm not feeling so well right now."

"Not feeling well," Sam repeated.

"Maybe coming down with something. I don't know."

"It's just that it seems like a shame to waste this food. Given that Alma cooked some extra for you and all. Maybe just a bite of mutton."

"I really don't . . ."

"Or some of those beans. Fresh from the garden."

Ted looked blankly down at his plate. He could feel them both watching him now. The room was completely quiet except for the tick of the clock on the wall.

"Eat it." Sam's voice was flat and hostile. "Eat the food."

"Sam . . . I just . . ." Ted started to stammer.

Sam roughly cut a piece of meat from his portion, his knife scraping harshly on the pewter plate. He skewered it with his fork.

"Eat what we put in front of you." He reached over and grabbed the front of Ted's shirt. Pulling him halfway across the table, he shoved the meat against his lips. "Go on, mister government man, eat our food."

"Sam, that's enough." Alma's voice cut through the room.

Sam released his grip on Ted and turned to her.

"What do we owe him?" he asked.

"He is our guest."

"He comes into our house. He tells us lies . . ."

"Now hold on there, Sam," Ted started.

"Shut up! Shut up!" Sam shouted at him. "You're not BLM. Anyone could see that. You're one of them AEC boys. One of them that come around here, telling us about the wonders of the atom. Operation Plowshare, right? Using the bomb to dig canals, make passes through the mountains. Like it says in the Bible, right? That the valleys will rise up and the mountains will be made low? You're one of them. We know what you are. And then, after all of this, you come here and you look at our food like it was poison . . ."

Ted put a smile on his face, humble, conciliatory, rueful. "Sam, I told you about that big lunch of mine. The food looks great, really." He cut a bite of his mutton and made a show of chewing it. "Now, that's good. Down-home cooking. Nothing like it."

Sam walked around the table and pulled Ted up by his shirt front. "You son of a bitch. Don't you talk down to me." He turned again to Alma. "Time for him to meet the rest of the family."

"Sam . . ." Her voice was exhausted, barely more than a whisper.

"Come on, mister. Mister BLM man. Come on upstairs and meet our son." He dragged Ted into the living room. The two of them struggled briefly, lurching up against the wall. But Sam was much stronger. He took a firm grip and dragged Ted like some recalcitrant farm animal up the stairs.

The room above was hot and dry, the coolness and moisture of the storm completely dissipated now, and the sun, even as it faded west, still blazing away outside. The two men were sweating, their chests heaving. The blinds were drawn against the sun, but in the dim light, Ted could make out a double bed with a figure reclining in it, shaking with labored, abrasive gasps.

"This is our son Bobby," Sam said. "Bobby, this is Ted. He's from the AEC."

The body on the bed twitched a little bit. As his eyes adjusted, Ted could see the boy better. He was tall, his legs stretched out to the end of the bed, but his limbs were thin and bony. He might have been in his late teens, but it was impossible to tell for sure. His belly was grotesquely distended under the threadbare sheet. The skin was stretched tight over his face, pulling his eyes and mouth open in a horrible expression of surprise. The room held a foul odor, like the den of a dying animal.

"He was out with the sheep during one of those tests. Those atomic tests," Sam said. "Told us there was a big flash of light and the ground shook. Half a day later something strange blew in—a gray, burnt-smelling fog that settled on his skin, stuff that wouldn't wash off with just water. His horse went down a couple days after he came back. Went down and didn't get up. Good horse. Just four years old. Laid down and died. And the sheep. The wool would come off in big clumps just touching them. Then Bobby got to feeling poorly. Couldn't keep anything down. Never been sick a day before."

The boy kept breathing that painful breath, each inhalation coming after a long pause that made you think it wasn't coming at all.

"We got a man from the atomic agency out here. Same man who gave us a program at the beginning. Telling us how safe everything was. How it was all scientific. Came back with some lawyers. Told us the sheep were dying of malnutrition. Now ain't that a heck of a thing? Our whole flock just up and dying of not eating right."

Bobby's stomach looked like he had swallowed a basketball. "It's been a long time coming, my son's death." Ted jumped at Alma's voice. She was right behind him. "He was a big, strapping boy, and that thing, whatever it is, it's taken a long time to suck the life out of him." She looked down at the boy for a second. "Long enough for me to stop praying for him to get better and start praying for him to die." Ted felt the sweat running down his face, but it offered no coolness in the hot, still room. "It takes a long time for a mother to get to that place, mister. He's been dying for longer than that. Long enough for me to stop praying altogether."

"You tell me about the future now, atomic man," Sam said. "You tell me about how bright the future is going to be. Either that or you get down on your knees and you help me pray that God will come and take my son." Sam was close enough for Ted to feel the man's breath on his face. He gagged at the rancher's breath, at the thick air in the room, at the combined smells of recently eaten food and death. He had a wild thought that he had never been so close to another human being in his life. Sam stayed there, staring at him, until Ted sank down to his knees by the bed.

Sam kneeled down next to him, and the two of them stayed like that for a long time, only the irregular, whistling sound of the boy's breath breaking the sweltering heat and darkness. They stayed still, kneeling there next to the bed, stayed until Ted's mouth went dry from the empty prayers, until his mind was barren of words. The two of them stayed there, silent and unmoving, stayed there still, like supplicants or worshippers or penitents, like midwives at the birth of something brand-new.

RICK KEMPA

Thirst and Water (excerpt)

The Man with No Sense of Space

Except for the swaggering, bragging sorts who frequent the corridor trails, where the air is permanently charged with bombast, I have met few hikers in the Grand Canyon who were not keepers of the silence. But memory of the ones whom I have met is etched in me, like dreams so outlandish that they steal your sleep.

There was, for instance, the man with no sense of space, who invaded my brother's and my campsite one evening early in a long trip. Returning from a little foray among the nearby cliffs, we were met by the astonishing sight of a big dome tent erected in a clearing no more than ten yards from where we'd pitched our tent. To say that this was out of the ordinary is to put it mildly. We were not, after all, in some roadside park with pull-in numbered sites, nor even in a designated backcountry campground. This was the huge Boucher Creek drainage system, spanning rim to river, encompassing a dozen side canyons and a hundred smaller drainages, a region to which the Park Service, with its perfect understanding that the canyon's greatest treasure is its emptiness, gives out only two camping permits per night, making it that much harder to *not* be alone. Indeed, this other tent was the first sign of man that we had seen since our hike began the previous day. It was deserted: its perpetrators, like us, having staked their claim and gone off to explore.

In turn I was incredulous, indignant, and morose over the intrusion— unable, as my city-wise brother began to counsel, to "adapt to it." I searched my own experience for an excuse for them. Fatigue, perhaps. One doesn't think clearly when the brain is gorged with blood. But cloudy thinking is one thing, and thoughtlessness another. "Maybe they're a couple of women who are here to make us happy," my brother offered, and although this made me smile, I couldn't manage a laugh. For it felt like a blockage in my breathing tube, this stranger's camp. Because of it, I would not be able to make the sounds I might otherwise make, nor even exist in quiet. As far as I was concerned, the presence of that one orange dome rearranged the space of the entire world.

And the person it belonged to filled that world. As it turned out, there were a group of four hikers, but only one counted: the leader, a manic Manhattanite whom I remember less for his appearance than for his emanations, the rigid lines of pulsing energy that jutted into everything. Even when he was not moving, he was moving—eyes darting, dodging, dilating, hands clutching, rearranging, feet twitching. And such a talker was he, louder than the ten thousand voices of Boucher Creek, that had the ghost of Louis Boucher, the hermit who lived out his life down there, been present, he would've bolted straightaway back to the city. He served up, unordered, a bottomless concoction of geologic data, historical tidbits, personal exploits, and informed predictions. Obviously fatigue was no excuse for him.

He would've made a better rock than a man, for so dense was he that he was unconscious of his intrusion. He got no message from my snubbing, and when I began to dismantle our tent (having realized the only sure way to escape him), he seemed to take at face value my brother's excuse for me, that we had found an even nicer campsite farther upstream.

Soon, filled with the buoyancy of the escape, my brother and I were guffawing at his expense. "Did you see how interested he seemed when you told him about our new campsite?" I asked, which made my brother suggest that we walk backwards, to throw him off our trail. And through our explorations in the days to come, in all the unlikeliest places where another person might be, a well-timed "don't look now, but here comes that guy again" would make us giddy with laughter.

My guffaws were in part a relief valve for worry, for in truth I feared him a little; it seemed not at all unlikely that he might nuzzle up to us again. We were, after all, traversing the same region as he was, and although the back country was huge, the water holes were scarce. Besides, hadn't he cried out after us, in that assured voice with which he said everything, "We'll catch you later"?

Days later he *did* catch us, on the beach of Bass Canyon, the far point of our hike. Sheets of rain had been buffeting us all night and morning, and it was nearly noon before we mustered the resolve to collapse our soggy tent and begin the climb up to the snow line, which was itself moving down to meet us. Working in concert, we pulled out the stakes and poles, shook and folded the fabric, and packed it away.

This was the moment when the man with no sense of space made his grand entry into canyon lore. He appeared at the crest of the low dune above our site, a dripping, grinning apparition. Those eyes of his were not trained on us, but rather over our shoulder at the dry rectangle of sand where our tent had been. He strode down to enter that space, paced the borders of it, and then like a pope blessing an acolyte for some small, imperfect deed, he said, "Not quite the right shape, but I can make it do." Throwing his head back he bellowed, "Hey you guys, come over here! Believe it or not, I found a dry place to set up!"

In that fog-shrouded air, his voice was muffled, diminished, although still plenty loud. We looked in the direction he had flung it. No sign whatsoever of his mates. But whether they were struggling up the backside of a nearby dune or wandering in a different side-canyon altogether, obviously he expected his voice to break upon them like thunder. Having once summoned them, he paid them no more mind.

His actions in themselves on that last day were appropriate enough. Any noninvasive move that keeps you drier in a storm is fair play, and if he could make our rectangle fit his circle, he was welcome to it. But I could not forgive the man for his voice. It had been nearly a week since our last encounter, ample time for him to be startled by his echo, to be disquieted, and quieted by it. Yet, incredibly, he had not heard.

As with the first time we left him, it was a pleasure to turn away; he made the storm seem suddenly like a refuge. But for his companions, who had no choice except to dwell within his space, we felt a surge of pity. For them, the spiritual dimension that is born in silence was denied. And without the enlarged perception that silence brings, without the vision of their small but steady progress against the shrouded cliffs, how could such a day as that, of needle-like rain, squishy feet, and clammy clothes, have been anything but an ordeal?

The Man who was a Storm unto Himself

Given time, the canyon can calm the storm in all of us. Maybe even the man with no sense of space would have been quieted, had he a season to spend there. Slowly you manage to still yourself, to let the silence be there in your ear. Blessedly, you put the map away for a while. You notice, and enjoy, how your erraticism has diminished, how your actions and bodily functions have settled into a rhythm. One morning you discover that your muscles don't hurt. The dive you take one afternoon into a river eddy or a water pocket of a creek feels like a baptism. Maybe there is an epochal moment, a little time spent out of time, an afternoon of gloriously aimless wandering, or an interval passed on a boulder at the rapid's edge, staring at how the water surges and surges by, and yet keeps the same shape.

Somewhere in the middle-ground of the hike, unrecognized at the time, is the turning point, measured not in terms of days or distances but internally. The sense begins to build in you that you got what you came for. This is almost always a premature thing, so you suppress it for awhile. But you begin to look towards the rim a little more frequently. *It is almost time*, you tell yourself. *Soon I will be ready.* Out comes the map.

Sometimes the forward impulse arrives so prematurely that whatever canyon experience you sought after is stillborn, that your dousing is not a baptism, but a mundane bath, worse than most. Some switch gets flicked, a button pushed that excludes the here-and-now, that hones in like a heat-seeking missile on the lone light on the rim, whether it is in view or not. Your actions become more a matter of reflex than reflection. It's entirely possible to wake up and find yourself five thousand vertical feet above the beach where you took your last rest.

I came upon the signs of one such flight early one morning in the Inner Canyon, as I was walking along a creek near which I'd camped. In the bed of gravel beside the creek, at the point where a trail cut across, lay three glistening mounds of some of the most delectable trail mix ever concocted. There was nothing accidental about this; the piles were too neat, too symmetrical to have been the result of a squirrel rampage or of spillage from a backpack pocket. The trail mix had been obviously and deliberately and unlovingly poured there. A thousand little bursts of taste and energy had become mere weight, impediment to speed. For me, it was a lucky find. I was the first browser on the scene; the dried fruit was only just beginning to swell in the moist air currents along the waterway, while the nuts were not yet damp enough to have lost their crunch. As I merrily scooped the piles into my own depleted GORP bag, I was conscious of how, somewhere not too far up trail, in the heat of his first sweat, someone was moving much faster than he intended to, wholly given over to the urge.

I met a person like him on another hike, a brother in flight, the man who was a storm unto himself. My partner Fern and I had spied him from a distance late one afternoon, striding through the willow-thickets along the river. He was the first person we'd seen in four days, so we watched him the way one watches any exotic species and amused ourselves with fantasies of bopping him over the head and stealing his food. He didn't hear our stifled giggles, so focused was he, and he would've chugged right on by, fifty yards distant, had I not hailed him. He staggered to a stop like one who had been shot and gaped at us. There was a bulge in his eyes and a slackness to his jaw of the heavily-worked or of the panicked. His face showed not even a hint of softening or gladness at meeting fellow humans. When at last he spoke, he uttered the most bizarre question I have ever heard come out of that place:

"Do you think the banks are open late on New Year's Eve?"

Fern and I were too astonished to speak. We were aware that it was New Year's Eve, for it had been a little goal of ours to save a tasty tidbit or two from our increasingly bland bag of food in order to celebrate. But as for the hours bankers keep! It took some groping before one of us could connect to that other world enough to make even a dumb response:

"You know, I really couldn't say."

He shook off the answer the way one shoos a fly; he needed something better than this to feed on.

"What about the telegraph office?" he demanded. "Can't you get money wired to you on holidays?"

I knew nothing about it, and I doubted it, but I was also beginning to know that this was a man in need of a good lie. "Yes," I told him, "I believe you can."

His lips came together over this, and his eyes narrowed to a point beyond us—the future, no doubt, and he with money in hand—for they were glowing. When they shifted back to us, it was to see us for the first time as people, instead of as information sources. And in the give-and-take world where his head resided, we required payment for our services. "You know," he said, letting his pack fall from his shoulders into the sand. "I need to lighten my load big time. I've got a bunch of crap in this pack that you might want."

We watched with suppressed excitement as he pawed through the pack's compartments. Out came packages of dried noodles, a bag of oatmeal, a couple of oranges (the sight of which made us salivate), and, most intriguing of all, two squeezable tubes filled with thick yellow goop. "Eggs," he told us, his voice edged with pride. He held one tube up to the light so that it glowed like liquid gold. "You see all that junk floating around in there? That's chopped onion, zucchini, and seasoning. Made it myself back in Cambridge."

For a moment his manic behavior ceased. Head cocked, eyes softening, he stared into the upheld tube, squeezing it with thumb and index so that the light rippled through it. It's easy to imagine what he was seeing: the Cambridge apartment, his last night in town, a few short hours before the flight west. All his gear still strewn on the living room floor, and he hunches over the cutting board, eyes burning as he minces the onion that will go into the tube.

His lover stirs on the couch. (Of course there is a lover; what else could have made him so crazed with hurry?) She taunts him: "Now what on earth are you doing?" And he, chuckling at the image of himself in her eyes: "I am making the best damned Colorado River breakfast ever to come out of Boston!"

He flung the tube into the sand at our feet. *Failure! Fuck up!* The air was thick with mute self-loathing. To think of the precious minutes spent weeping over onions when they could've been in each other's arms! And look at him now—so sick with missing her, so weak that he was blinded to everything but the image of her alone on New Year's Eve, or, worse, not alone.... It was stupid, but he couldn't help it, he had to know. He absolutely had to find a phone. "Baby, it's me. Yeah, I know it's a surprise, things changed. Don't ask questions. Just talk to me."

But what the hell would he do if she wasn't home? Even before he was done hoisting his pack he was on the move, calling over his shoulder, "You can take the shit, or you can leave it for the fucking mice."

We took the shit of course, and like any fucking mouse would do, we ate it all that night, except for the oatmeal. We had a lip smacking, slap-me-five good time too, reliving with delight and disbelief how our fantasies of snatching his food had come true, and without the clubbing! But whenever we sobered, the thought returned that sharing this same big space with us was a tortured man whom, lightened load aside, we had met and not helped.

Of course he had not made it out of the canyon. It seemed a physical impossibility, that one could hike fourteen miles, in addition to however far he'd already hiked, five thousand feet uphill, nonstop, mostly in darkness, much of it through snow. Maybe his anguish would make him superhuman and, sometime during the first hours of the New Year, he would reel onto the road. What then? The trail head was another five miles from the nearest phone. No, he would not place his call that night. We hoped he had realized this, and had put his miserable head to rest. We wished him a New Year that was not "happy," but not so loud either, that he would wake into the quiet, almost leaden calmness that millions of revelers the world over would wake to, and that he would recognize his advantage over them, namely *where he was*, and that he would find whatever food he had not cast off and take time to eat and digest, and become more like himself.

I know him because I have been him. I have been on the trail in the first light of dawn when, according to the plan as written on the permit dangling from my pack, I should've been lolling in my tent, slowly waking to a day of lovely aimlessness. I am famous for putting the last two days' hikes into one, no matter how long the hikes or short the days; for casting it as a conscious choice instead of the blind flight it really was; for emphasizing the wonder of it, how very far one could hike in a single day, and ignoring the sad truth, how very little I saw along the way; for concocting a test to fit the result: "I wanted to see what my limits were," instead of simply admitting that I failed to stay as long as I planned. I have made the midnight call to my own Dulcinea del Toboso and heard the stunned, slightly cranky, not-at-all-angelic voice whose absence drove me mad. I have learned to live with the aftertaste of false excuses, and more importantly, I have learned how to accept it.

Into the Calm

One person among all whom I've encountered in my four decades of canyon hiking exists in memory as he who was at home there. In his eyes, his bearing, in the *presentness* he exuded, it was clearly written he had been somewhere mere distance could not measure.

I met him fleetingly in the middle of a switchback-ridden slope of a rim-to-river trail. From above I watched him approach: a lean figure bent slightly forward against the steep slope, his long legs taking every obstacle in stride, keeping the same pace. Obviously not just *in shape* but *in sync*, he seemed to be gliding rather than climbing. His fluidity was marvelous to behold, for I, at the outset of my own hike, was jump-starting and stalling my way downhill, still feeling for my first rhythms.

As he neared, I called out a greeting. He glanced up from the moving patch of earth on which he had been focused and gave a small nod. His face towards me was neither open nor closed; he took me in, as one would take in a large boulder that had settled on the trail (for I was standing in the middle of it), then he stepped off and around me on the downslope. I recognized that he was not being rude, that he was simply *in motion*. Nonetheless, I wanted more from him. He was emerging from a region where I had never been, where I was about to spend a week, and where, because it was midwinter, I would quite possibly meet no one else. The exploratory spirit that I had been nurturing dissolved before this information source. My questions stopped him short.

Yes, I would find water in the side canyons; there had been plenty of rain. Yes, there would be overhangs to sleep under if I looked around enough. (His voice lacked all variation in tone or pitch, as if he had forgotten those human tricks; he was a mere transmitter of facts.) Yes, I could get down to the river in some of the canyons—he named them—but if it was raining, I ought to watch out for flash floods. At this, his eyes clouded over, and he shifted them away. He seemed to feel he'd said too much, moving past information to the realm of advice. Who was he to tell someone what to undertake or not? Wasn't it after all a perfectly fine way to die, in the first swell of a flood? With another nod, he abruptly dismissed himself.

I came to know him better in the week that followed, during the course of my own journey into the rain-soaked rhythms of that world. Each side canyon where I made my camp had, as he'd foretold, the perfect overhang—tall enough to sit upright or sometimes even stand, deep enough to stretch out my sleeping bag and still be dry. As he'd said, the shelter took some finding. Sometimes it was upstream, sometimes down, and always it was hidden in the cliffs above the creek bed. But I always recognized it, for it was the one with the level bed of sand, the little rock-wall windbreak, and the small, neat pile of kindling. After awhile I knew him well enough to not stop looking until I found the kindling.

In the evenings, as I huddled in my room of rock, warming my toes, drying my boots and socks, and quieting myself by my small, fierce fire, I was less alone because of him. For it was *his hands* that pruned the wood from the wetness, *his fire* that dried it, it was he who neatly stacked that wood with thought of me in mind. He, like me, had sat behind the curtain of water streaming from the rocks above, watching the cliffs drift in and out amidst the fog.

Neither was he alone, for the wood of his fire had been gathered, dried, and stacked by hands before his. He had seemed so strong, so entirely self-possessed in our one true encounter. But maybe as he nurtured his first fires down here, his spirit was as fragile as mine, his capacity for solitude as tenuous. Maybe he too needed the thought of others in order to ride out the storm waves of self, in order to come into the calm. This is how ordinary men and women are able to withstand themselves, by moving across time to join hands.

No voices, please. Let our poor heads be at rest. Let the silence and the solitude be tangibles. A rock or two of the windbreak wall has been put in place by each of us. I too find a rock that fits.

GROWTH
AND RESURGENCE

RICK KEMPA

The Burn, Four Years After

(*for Fern*)

i.
The deadfall, the tangle of chokecherry, scrub oak, nettles—
signs of a forest's wealth, but also of its clutter:
this is gone. All that's left are charred tree trunks,
stripped, as if hewn from above, of their foliage,
countless black votive candles offered to the light that,
unimpeded at last, inundates the forest floor.
Reveling in it now, we realize
the sky is what we missed most, the clouds
massing above the peaks, a milky dreaminess,
and this astonishing light.

The forest was too thick anyway, you assert,
always turning in upon itself, too green,
too difficult to move there, to breathe even,
an accumulation so insistent that the details,
this tree, *this* nest, were lost.

ii.
Of the fire itself, nothing was ever written.
Like the blueprint of a fruit in a charred seed,
words were incinerated before they could take shape.
Summoned one bleak morning to the fire line,
our task instead was brute survival,
our lives forged by what transpired.

iii.
I am struck by the fire's randomness:
how for acres and acres there is only this black death,
and then, for no visible reason, no fortuitous placement

in the middle of a meadow, or in a gully over which
the firestorm leapt, or in the lee of a hill that took the brunt,
one fir tree stands, shriven but intact.

iv.
You are the one against whom the odds
were piled so high that by rights they should have
crushed you, the one with the lucky seat
in the back of the doomed plane,
she who was pulled out alive from the rubble
ten days after the quake.

When you came back we wanted to know
not just how you were, but *who*—
as if you had fallen from your horse and seen God,
as if you should have a new name.

You want to say you're not so different,
that each of us always is equally close to death.
Your skirmish was just more public, more prolonged,
an amateur high-wire act without nets.

The difference you feel is from the person you were
before the burn, when the canopy of your mind
teemed with a lushness all its own,
when continuity like a first-growth forest
anchored you securely to your roots.
I have seen your mouth open in disbelief:
How can a language just disappear? Where does it go?
I have seen you turn your back to hide the fear:
*How can something that has undergone
such a burn still be beautiful?*

v.
Yes, it regenerates, each season grows more lush.
Again deer browse here in the hour before dawn,
bear score the trees with their signatures, and
the drama of the ground squirrels has resumed.

But up in the canopy, light exposes absence.
Gone is the blue flash of the Steller's jay,
the sparrow's explosion into flight,
the warbler's complicated frame—
that which you loved the most.
Instead, deadwood soughs in the wind,
and the black-hooded raven makes its rounds.

It took this long to recognize the error in our thinking:
No matter what time span we allow,
the forest will never be the same.

vi.
We are supposed to think of it as a tragedy:
Such a loss! Such an absence of what was!
That is why, walking with you through the burn
this summer morning four years after,
with the yellow light suffusing everything
and the broad leaves of the new growth shimmering
and the colonies of wild flowers shaking off their sleep—

when our hearts quicken and our blood surges
so that we are dizzy, either hot or cold,
we can't tell which—the word that rises
to our lips seems somehow incorrect,
yet here it is: how *beautiful!*

vii.

And you, dropping to your knees to inspect a flower,
exclaiming in wonder, calling me to see
how each of its five petals has a light blue fringe
that flushes rose, then scarlet, and how from its
brilliant yellow center five white anthers curl—

Kneeling beside you, I am witness to still more:
the golden fleck of pollen on your nose,
the russet hue of fireweed on your cheeks,
open sky mirrored in your eyes . . .

I am here to tell you that
a forest is no less itself
merely because it has burned.

WILLIAM CASS

The Luckiest Boy in the World

P aul lived with his family in a cluster of Native housing a few miles from the village of Yakutat, Alaska, out between the airport and the road to Coast Guard Lake and Cannon Beach. Theirs was one of a dozen or so pre-fab houses that had been built a decade before in the late sixties at the edge of a wide meadow just up from the weather station. Paul's grandmother's place was a few houses away, and his uncle's family's was just around the bend in the other direction. When he stood at his bedroom window, which he often did, Paul looked out over the wide, green-grey meadow and the tall weather tower to the side of it with its blinking red light as ever-present as the grease that sat in the skillet on his grandmother's stove.

Dense green-black spruce forest stood like a dark wall at the far reaches of the meadow where it became bog. The gravel road to the lake and the beach ran like a blade cut through the trees until it reached the driftwood-covered dunes and ocean, wild and windswept now in the fall that stretched untouched and uninhabited for hundreds of miles in each direction. Just to the north, Yakutat Bay interrupted the ocean briefly and the central part of the village sat on the hillside above it, the cannery on one end and the boat harbor on the other. Across from the harbor was the thin strip of Khantaak Island, and beyond that in the distance, the St. Elias range, the highest coastal mountain range in the world that swept east and south in a continuous semi-circle until it met the Tsongas National Forest. Mt. St. Elias loomed at the near end, its peak like a huge incisor tooth so high in the sky that it still seemed impossible to Paul on those seventy or so times a year when the rain or snow stopped long enough for it to be visible. Even at the height of the brief summer months, its charcoal crevices were always streaked with snow, and its sharp tip remained brilliant white year-round. If there was a gateway to the range, it would have been Yakutat, but the village was so remote, tucked in the corner where southeastern Alaska met its larger portion, that few people had ever set foot anywhere near it. By area, it was one of the largest cities in the world, six times the size of Rhode Island, but the only way into it was by boat or plane. The long distances and forbidding seas made the former nearly impossible, so it was generally reached via air by one of the two daily stops that Alaska Airlines made for refueling or by arranging a flight with one of the few guides who operated their own float planes.

Most of the other Native housing, except for the small section along the inland road to the dump and the glacier, clung to the hillside above the Tlingit lodge, the general store, and the health clinic, adjacent to the post office, the two restaurants, and the bar. All but a smattering of the three hundred Natives lived in housing. A few had married outsiders and lived in cabins and trailers scattered here and there. Perhaps fifty other outsiders had moved there at one time or another, too—teachers at the school, some Coast Guard, weather station, Fish and Game personnel, and a couple dozen commercial fisherman, guides, or cannery workers.

Like almost all of the Natives in the village, both Paul's father and mother held gill netting permits and depended on the majority of their yearly income from subsistence salmon fishing from May to October at their fish camps near the mouths of the Situk and Lost Rivers. When there was a steady run, which was often the case in those years of unspoiled and rich fishery, and the price for salmon was high, a good season could yield twenty to thirty thousand dollars per permit. So, with a decent Permanent Fund Dividend check and a freezer stocked with salmon, halibut, crab, shrimp, and whatever hunting season provided, a family could get by all right. That was especially the case if a few of the men with tags killed a moose during the annual short opening and divided the meat among relatives, as was the Tlingit tradition.

At twelve, Paul was a number of years away from a moose hunt and still several away from getting his gill net permit, but was nearing the time when boys in the village were more often given their first shotgun, something he'd longed for above anything else since he was in kindergarten. That was the first year his father and uncle had allowed him to accompany them on their goose and duck hunts. Although he loved fishing and anything else to do with the outdoors, there was something magical to Paul about those early morning trips alone with the older men. He would already be awake in the darkness and waiting when his father came quietly into his bedroom to touch his shoulder while his two younger brothers slept in their bunk beds across from him. He dressed in a smaller version of the same camouflage coveralls and vest that his father and uncle did, the same brown knit cap, the same green Gortex shell if it was raining, and he carried his own small knapsack with variations of the same contents theirs held: a thermos of hot chocolate, dried salmon, binoculars, and an old decoy that they rarely used. When he came into the kitchen, the single yellow light over the sink would be piercing the inky blackness as his father filled their knapsacks at the counter. Paul would walk over to the table and touch the spongy case that held his father's shotgun. Their yellow lab, Daisy, would be scratching and whining softly at the back door in anticipation, especially as the crawl of his uncle's truck tires approached and its headlights swept across them through the kitchen window. Then he'd be sitting between his father and uncle in the truck cab with the heater warming his knees as they rode in close silence to one of their blinds in the marshes along Coast Guard Lake.

His uncle would have set the decoys and they would be settled in the blind before first light, his father and uncle positioned at the front, and Paul behind them holding Daisy as she panted and whimpered. Unless there was a stream or river nearby, that was the only sound until the initial hint of pink-grey licked the treetops to the east and his uncle put the tiny horn to his lip for his opening call. At the sound, Paul always felt the same flood of excitement and leaned forward, reaching for the stick that he would use to track the birds' flight as his father knelt and steadied his gun on the lip of the blind. Waiting between calls, a softer feeling of awe, familiarity, and gladness spread over him as this great wilderness that was his home slowly unfolded with the gathering wash of dawn.

With no permanent police officer and only the two Fish and Game wardens in the village, liberties were taken and overlooked in respect to some laws and regulations. So, although the legal age for waterfowl hunting tags was sixteen, most boys there learned to handle a shotgun earlier than that, as they did a four-wheeler or a snowmobile. Paul's father and uncle had begun teaching him that spring in the meadow behind his house. First, they'd set out tin cans on a fifty-gallon drum at increasing distances. Then his uncle would kneel behind the drum out in the meadow and throw Frisbees as high and far as he could while his father coached Paul as he tracked and shot at them. After all of his time studying things in the blind and practicing in the meadow, Paul's aim quickly became passable.

His birthday fell on the second Wednesday in October, and when he came home from school that afternoon, he found his father and uncle sitting on the living room couch drinking beer with a new shotgun lying on its case on the coffee table in front of them. There was a red bow taped to its barrel and two brown boxes of shells in shrink-wrapped cellophane next to it.

The two men stopped talking as Paul entered the room and looked at him expectantly. They smiled as his eyes widened and he put a hand to his cheek.

"Well?" his father said.

Paul shook his head. "Mine?"

"If you care for it right. No shooting unless you're with one of us."

"Sure," he said. He dropped his knapsack of school books on the floor and ran his finger along the gun's shiny handle. "Can I?" he stammered. He looked back and forth at the two men. "Can I . . ."

His uncle sat forward and lifted the burlap sack of Frisbees at his feet. "Come on," he said.

His father stood up and handed Paul the new gun. "Remember. Not unless you're with one of us."

Paul nodded and stared down at the delicious heft in his hands.

His father ruffled Paul's hair and said, "Let me get my coat."

* * *

Paul bragged about the gun to his mother and grandmother at dinner, and to his friends in the housing cluster. His younger brothers and cousins also paid it some admiration. But his father and uncle left on a trawler pulling two skiffs with some other men the next afternoon to go seal hunting up near Icy Bay where one of the men had a cabin. They didn't know how long they'd be gone, but it might be a week, maybe longer. So, his first trip to the blind sat just beyond Paul's reach, and with only a few more weeks before the waterfowl began migrating, this became more and more tantalizing and frustrating with each passing day.

While they were gone, Paul oiled and cleaned the gun every afternoon after school and slept with it under his bed. He often took it out after his brothers had fallen asleep and practiced loading and unloading it in the moonlight that came through the bedroom window.

One morning, he arose very early to the first snowfall of the year and took the gun into the hallway. He paused at his parents' doorway and waited to be sure his mother was still sleeping, and then crept into the kitchen. After he'd pulled his coveralls over his pajamas and his boots over his bare feet, he opened the back door slowly so it wouldn't squeak. Daisy roused herself from the basket there where she slept, regarded him, and began panting. Paul put his index finger to his lips and shook his head to her, and then let himself out the door, closing it slowly behind him. He walked quietly on the soft snow out to the woodshed twenty or so yards away, where he set the gun gently against the entry. He rearranged the logs on the open side facing the meadow until there was a section that approximated the dimensions of a blind, and he knelt down behind it. He curled his left hand into the shape of a horn and blew a soundless call, then lifted the gun to the ledge of the logs, adjusted the butt until it rested comfortably against his right shoulder and did the same with the comb against his face, sighted along the barrel out into the moonlit meadow and whispered the sound of it firing, puffing from his cheeks, and allowing it an imaginary recoil. As much as it made his heart race, it made it ache even more.

An afternoon came early the following week when Paul felt his heart stir again, but in a different way. He'd just come home from school to an empty house. His father was still away on the seal hunt, and his mother had left a note saying that she and his brothers had gone to a cousin's baby shower in the village and would be home by dinnertime. That meant he had at least two hours ahead of him that would be unencumbered and unsupervised.

He hurried into his room, took the gun out from under the bed, sat it on his desk, and rubbed the pebbly surface of its stock. He looked out the window and across the snow-covered meadow toward the line of trees. The light had already begun its fall towards evening.

"I'll go for a ride," he said aloud. "I'll go down to the lake to see if it's frozen yet. I'll take the gun in case of emergency. In case I have to fire off a warning shot if I come upon a bear or I have to shoot off signals if I blow a tire. For safety. That's what I'll do."

Before he allowed his mind to consider further, he'd packed the gun and some shells in its case and was heading out to the woodshed where they kept the four-wheeler. He lashed the case on the back with bungee cords, then started the engine and drove off across the meadow and onto the road to Coast Guard Lake.

The track was empty; there was no reason for anyone to be on it in late October in the dwindling light of day. He shifted easily until he was in fourth gear and then sped along, the rear tires throwing two plumes of snow behind him, and his breath coming in short clouds against the cold. He wished he'd worn a cap.

Paul reached the lake in less than twenty minutes, parked, unstrapped the gun, took it out of its case, and carefully loaded it with two shells. The barrel made a satisfying click as he snapped it into place. He secured the safety and carried it out in front of him with the stock at one hip and the barrel pointed diagonally in the other direction as he'd seen his father and uncle do.

He walked down to the water's edge. A thin layer of ice had formed along the lip of the lake, but that was all. The rest of it sat black and wide and perfectly still against the ring of untouched snow along its banks and the cavern of dark trees that surrounded it. It was so quiet that he could hear himself breathe through his nose.

Paul followed the path around the long curve of the lake to the shallows where it met the wide stream that flowed from it. Lily pads spread across the inlet there, and he studied the places where he'd caught cutthroat trout and where they'd seen a black swan remain alone into November two years before. He stopped where the path started through the woods to their first blind.

A sudden rustle high in the trees startled him. Instinctively, he raised the gun and fired it at the sound. A bald eagle called and flew off above its nest in the charred treetop where he'd aimed, and he heard a soft thud in the undergrowth below it. Paul blinked several times. The sweat that had risen on the back of his neck grew cold as the echo of the eagle's calls dissipated in the distance. He dropped the gun in the snow and ran to where he'd heard the thud.

Paul came upon the eaglet immediately after entering the stand of trees. Perhaps eight inches in length, it lay on its side in the thick moss. Blood trickled from its breast, but its heart was still beating, and one of its eyes followed him as he crept up to it. He put his hand over his mouth and whispered, "No." He shook his head and said more loudly, "No, no, no, no!"

He knelt beside the bird and began to cry.

Light fell more quickly in that dense canopy of growth as Paul lowered his head to his knees and shook it. Finally, he wiped the snot away from his face, sniffed, and swallowed hard. He forced himself to consider options. He looked quickly at the eaglet again; it was exactly the same: its heart beating quickly, blood oozing from several spots in its breast, its eye staring directly at him.

"I can't bury it alive," he said. "I can't bring it home. And I can't leave it here like this. I can't."

His heart thudded as he looked around him, found a piece of bark nearby, and slid it under the eaglet. He carried it over to the stream and set the bark down gently in the current. The eaglet kept its eye on him as the bark spun once and then was swept to the middle where it gained speed. Paul watched it until it disappeared around the bend into the murky dimness.

He stomped his way back through the devil's club and fiddleheads to where he'd left the gun, pumped the shells free from it, and threw them with a grunt as deep as possible into the woods. He didn't look at the unloaded shotgun as he carried it at his side back to the four-wheeler, where he lashed it on the back, and drove home. The four-wheeler's headlight pierced the full darkness that fell as he drove and lit the wisps of snow that had begun to fall. He choked back sobs several times before he'd returned the four-wheeler to the woodshed and the shotgun under his bed. He climbed under the covers in his clothes without turning on the light.

Paul's mother and brothers returned a while later. When his mother came into his room to get him for dinner, he told her he didn't feel well. She came over to him in the darkness and he felt the back of her hand against his forehead. "You're not hot," she said.

He just shook his head. After a few moments, he heard the door close behind her.

It was a number of hours later and long after the rest of the house had grown still that he finally fell into a fitful sleep. He rose early the next morning so that he could avoid any of them and get out to the bus stop early.

He sat away from where the other students would gather, slumped over, hugging himself.

* * *

Paul's father and uncle came home a few days later and planned their first goose hunting trip with him for the following Saturday. When his father came to rouse him that morning, he was already sitting dressed on the edge of the bed biting a thumbnail, the shotgun zipped in its case next to him.

"Ready?" his father whispered.

Paul shrugged.

"Let's go then, big fella."

He asked to sit in the back of the truck with Daisy and held the dog's warm head on his lap, scratching her behind the ears, as they bounced along the gravel road. The snow had melted and a fine rain began to fall that he hardly noticed.

When they got to the blind and had set out the decoys, his father and uncle arranged Paul between them and then helped him ready his gun along the ledge.

His uncle glanced at his father and they left their own guns on the ground. Softly, his father said, "The first shot is yours alone."

The rain had been replaced by a light mist that crept along the tall reeds out in front of them and the black brackish water beyond them. Paul wiped the sweat from his palms on the legs of his coveralls and swallowed over the tightness in his throat. Traces of dawn had just begun to show through the treetops when his uncle made his first call, and an explosion of flapping wings near the decoys followed it. A bevy of geese rose quickly, honking. Paul followed their flight with the barrel of his gun and sighted as he'd been taught, then hesitated for the second he hoped was brief enough not to be noticed, and fired behind the birds.

The bevy was soon a cluster of specks in the gray light. Daisy whined and pawed frantically behind him, but Paul's father held her by the collar.

"Shh," he quieted the dog. "Shh. Not now. Not this time."

"Shucks," Paul said. He kept his stare straight ahead where the birds had been.

"It's okay," his uncle said. "It took me two or three times before I got my first."

Paul's father chuckled and said, "It took you a hell of a lot longer than that."

His uncle laughed, too, and told Paul, "We'll give you the next one alone, too. Then you get in line and take turns like the rest of us."

Paul hoped his own small smile looked as sheepish as he'd intended. While he reloaded the gun, he tried not to think of the eaglet. But the image of it kept creeping into his mind, lying on its side in the moss and floating away down the stream on the bark, always with its one eye gazing at him.

His next shot didn't come for almost an hour. As he'd planned, Paul fired early and high over the birds before they had established their line of flight. They flew off to the east again, small scratches against the low gray clouds that promised the resumption of rain.

His father held Daisy again while she panted and whined. Paul lowered his barrel slowly, shaking his head and mumbling. He heard his uncle snap his own shotgun into place and watched him rest the barrel on the ledge of the blind. His uncle handed him the call horn.

"Wait a little while, and then like we practiced," he said. "Low and long."

Paul took the horn but avoided his uncle's eyes.

"Don't worry," he heard his father say, and then felt his hand on his shoulder. "Your time will come."

The full morning had passed and rain had soaked completely through their Gortex shells before they quit. During that time, they'd changed blinds twice. Daisy had retrieved two birds for his father and one for his uncle, and Paul had misfired on three additional shots. On their way back to the truck, he carried the birds in the mesh sling across one shoulder, the most recently shot goose in it still warm against his hip in contrast to the chill in his chest.

* * *

On the next goose hunting morning, Paul stalled in the house, saying he wanted to add an extra pair of socks to his knapsack, so his father and uncle were already in the cab of the idling truck ready to leave when he carried his gear outside. He set the shotgun in its case on the ground behind the truck, opened the tailgate, and tossed his knapsack inside. Then he hopped in the bed, closed the tailgate, took up his spot sitting against the back window of the cab, and whistled for Daisy. The dog shuffled over against his leg as Paul's uncle began to back up out of the drive. Even in the gravel, the bump and crunch of metal were evident as the back passenger side rear tire went over the gun. His uncle stopped the truck abruptly, and the two men jumped out of the cab as Paul did the same from the back. The stock end of the gun's case extended out from under the truck.

"I'm so stupid," Paul said. "I forgot to put it up in back before I closed the tailgate."

His father knelt down, pulled the case free from under the wheel well, and unzipped it. There was enough of the waning moon to show the flattened and twisted barrel, the ring around the trigger bent at ninety degrees, and both sights broken off completely. His father looked up at Paul, and he could feel his uncle's eyes on him, too.

"I'm sorry," Paul told them. He kept his eyes on the gun. "I'm so sorry. It's my fault. I'll work and pay for it."

His father slowly re-zipped the case and handed it up to Paul. He said, "It was an accident."

Paul tried to cry, but no tears would come, even when he forced himself to think of the eaglet.

"Well," his uncle said. "I guess you could still come along if you want. Sit in the blind, take a turn."

Paul shook his head, turned, and walked to the house. Inside the back door, he waited until he heard the truck's doors close and its tires gain speed on the road before he closed his eyes and blew out a breath of relief.

* * *

He found a job later that week washing dishes at the airport diner. Although he wasn't old enough to be hired formally, the owner had been good friends with both of his dead grandfathers, and said he'd pay Paul to come clean breakfast dishes on weekends. So, he began that, often riding the four-wheeler up the road to the airport as his father and uncle were heading out to hunt, which helped resolve two issues.

But the memory of the eaglet wouldn't go away. Nor the dreams from which he'd startle himself awake in a cold sweat and the sleeplessness that followed. Nor the pang he felt seeing a bear with its cub, or a cat with its kitten, or a mother, like the cousin who'd had the baby shower, with her newborn. Nor the slow ache that spread over him abruptly and often at the awe of the natural world around him—the perfect, still whiteness of the meadow in the early morning after a night of snow; the return of the humpback whales outside the bay in the early spring; the blue sheets of glacier calving into Harlequin Lake as the melt-off began in early summer or, during its longest days, the identical pink hues low on both horizons after midnight as the sun set in the west and rose in the east; or the red flanks on the last of the silver salmon in late September beginning to crust white in the shallow portion of the river at Nine Mile Bridge, their tails waving slowly, grudgingly waiting to die, too weary any longer to make the leap up the short falls on the other side. Things like these, their rhythms—as well as his own place in them and what he'd taken from them—tugged at Paul's heart more quietly as time passed, it seemed to him, but more endlessly.

That didn't change until his grandmother had her stroke early the following summer. Paul's uncle found her on that afternoon lying by the side of her bed where she'd fallen when first stricken upon rising that morning.

She was medi-vacked to Juneau. His father and uncle took turns flying in to stay with her at the hospital there. Several weeks passed before his uncle returned from a rotation and he could hear him, his aunt, his mother, and his father talking around the kitchen table late at night. Paul was already lying awake after one of his dreams and listened to them discuss the alternatives for his grandmother. The doctors had been clear that she could no longer care for herself, so these basically boiled down to placing her in the nursing home in Juneau or having her come home to live with one of them. His uncle and aunt had two very young children of their own, so neither family had room for her. And the flights to Juneau were expensive and infrequent, to say nothing of the cost of the nursing care. They didn't speak regarding how they'd feel about her living alone, away from her home for her remaining years, or how she would feel about that herself, but Paul thought about it listening to them, and from their long silences, he knew that they all did, too.

An idea came to him there in the dark, forming slowly, until he sat up straight. Something he hadn't felt in a long time released in him suddenly, something that had to do with hope.

He got up and walked into the kitchen. They stopped talking and sat looking at him standing there in his pajamas and with disheveled hair, his hands at his side, his eyes clear and steady.

"I'll live with her," he said, "and take care of her. You can take turns helping when I'm at school. I can make her meals, feed her, bathe her, dress her, find her something to watch on TV, read to her, get her in and out of bed. I can listen to her stories about Grandpa and the old days. I'll make jigsaw puzzles with her. Be with her, and get one of you if there's an emergency. I can do all of those things."

They sat around the table saying nothing, fingering their coffee cups. Then they began exchanging glances until their eyes all fell back on him. It remained silent until Paul said again, "I can do all of those things. I can, and I will."

* * *

Paul's father helped him move a few of his belongings into the spare bedroom at his grandmother's house the next morning before leaving on the plane to Juneau. He returned with her on the late afternoon flight the following day. Paul had cleaned her house and set out some wildflowers he'd gathered from the meadow in a vase on the coffee table: lupine and fireweed. The rest of the family had gone out to meet the plane, and after he heard it land, he stood in the open front doorway and waited. It had been rainless for almost a full week, and as the two trucks approached, dust lifted behind each on the gravel road. It settled gradually as they parked, and the sun was lowering in the cloudless sky beyond them. Paul's grandmother sat between his father and mother in the cab of the first truck. His mother got out first on the passenger side, and helped his grandmother climb down carefully and deliberately while his father brought her new walker from the truck bed around to her. His uncle's family and his brothers soon gathered around her.

She didn't begin towards the house right away, nor look at Paul in the doorway. Instead, she gazed slowly around her in all directions, out across the meadow, up and down the road, around the scattering of houses, then up at the weather station tower and the wide blue expanse above it. Paul watched her close her eyes, tap the fingertips of one hand against her lips, and inhale deeply. She seemed to smile from one side of her face.

Finally, she began to make her way up to the house, leaning the walker first one way, then the other. His father carried her suitcase, his uncle kept a protective hand stretched out behind her, and the rest of the family shuffled alongside until they reached the front step and she looked up at Paul.

She hadn't even been gone a full month, but she appeared more gaunt and frail to him than before, shrunken smaller than himself. Her white hair had been recently permed, and he could see her small skull through it. She reached her hand up to him and he took it. His uncle moved the walker to the side as Paul helped her up the one step and into the doorway next to him where their eyes met. Hers danced merrily and her mouth moved in a chewing motion that trembled.

From a side of it, she mumbled, "Thank you."

It was difficult to understand her, but he nodded and smiled.

"We'll be good pals," she whispered and patted his arm. "You and I."

* * *

Summer eventually gave way to the hint of fall, with its lingering paces, which mirrored those of Paul and his grandmother together. As the days began to shorten, she often liked to sit out back in lawn chairs before bed with a shawl over her knees as the sun began to settle behind the trees. Paul sat next to her; sometimes he read to her, but more often, they simply sat in silence looking out over the meadow in the falling light while she took his hand. At times, they saw a bear or moose out at the far edges where the bog met the tree line, and there were frequently birds—ravens, geese, ducks, egrets—that lifted and flew off through the inky light of the gloaming.

As time went on, Paul's heart clenched less and less strongly at the sight of the birds. It was as if someone had soundlessly and gradually massaged away a tender spot there. The times when he awoke, startled from a bad dream, became only occasional. Paul left shotgun money for his father in intervals until he felt it had been paid for, and circumstances with his grandmother's care negated any further suggestions of his joining in their hunting trips again. Paul was thankful for that. He was thankful for his life—for all of it, the way things had unfolded and the opportunities he'd been given. Sitting quietly next to his grandmother in that wild, vast place that was his home, Paul felt incredibly fortunate. He felt like he was the luckiest boy in the world.

SCOTT T. STARBUCK

Truant

At twelve, I wanted salmon fishing
over Catholic school,

gob of boraxed eggs flung
in silver current

for a giant sea slab
of tugging beet-red flesh.

Father Vince said he would make me
a fisher of men

but I chose instead to be
a fisher of fish.

Once, a police officer stopped
the vet who mentored me.

"Isn't that boy
supposed to be in school?" he asked.

"Well, he is in school," said the vet,
smiling like a drunk cowboy.

"Yes, I guess he is," said the cop.

DAVID LAVAR COY

Fear of Electricity

Our buckskin stallion
feared the electric fence
so much it would not enter
the pasture through the opened gate.
It had been shocked once
and would not be stung again.

So what do you do
when you are ten and
the stallion refuses command,
faces you down and slips on past?
You can follow behind and yell,
"Come back, come back."

Which doesn't do a thing.
The horse disappears
down the lane, and you go home
with your failure to explain
to a father who can't understand
because to him failure is no option.

He grabs his shotgun,
gathers up his sons, you being one,
in the back of the pickup, drives
everywhere he can, looking
for the rogue stallion. His plan
is to scare it

into the neighbor's corral,
which he manages to do, after hours
on the run, with some buckshot
pumped into its rear-end.
He slows it down,
but does not make it calm.

Suddenly, you find yourself standing
with your hand on the opened
metal gate, blocking the animal's
route of escape, letting
the horse's size and strength
incite you to terror.

Until your father explains,
in a rather loud whisper, "Son,
he'll see your fear.
He's looking for weakness.
Turn around calmly,
and lock the damn gate."

DAVID LAVAR COY

Blackouts on the Ranch

Doorknobs are like handshakes,
You are glad to meet them.
Glad for pegs to hang your coat on
glad the bed, when you open
its covers, is a familiar story.
Once you light candles,
you are living the old-time rural lifestyle
when darkness made the edges
of the world fuzzy, and people lived
within circles: lantern, moon,
flashlight, candle light.
Remember being halted
by the sudden extinction of flame,
when the candle blew out?
The fumble for a match? After
you struck it, joy recovered its balance.
No one needs the whole picture
all of the time, just enough light
to make one step at a time
without serious stumbling.
A candle's enough light
to milk a cow by, though once
a local farmer set a haystack on fire.

MICHAEL HARTY

Hoarding the Rain

They have gone now, the lean old men
who remembered, whose pale cobwebbed eyes
had watched cowhands with mule teams
scrape to save water, mound up
earthen dams across shallow washes,
spread clay to block seepage, form
one by one the ponds you see now
from miles high, reflecting sunset
like gold coins scattered across a table.

They'd seen the ponds fill, cattle
wading belly-deep, lush grass below the dam
where before it took five acres
to feed one cow. The old men's eyes
took in abundance, but hardship
was in their bones. Their skin
would always be leather
and they were not surprised
when it was a long time between rains.

BENJAMIN DANCER

Time Out of Mind

Are you still in AP English?" Tim waited to ask his daughter the question until after dinner. Julie had been staying with her boyfriend, and Tim felt too fragile to risk losing a few minutes with her at the table. He hadn't seen his son in days, and just yesterday he received a text from Teri, his wife, requesting another meeting, which meant the divorce papers were prepared and ready to be signed.

Julie lied to him. "Yeah."

They were washing the dishes together.

It felt to Tim like his life had been taken away. He didn't blame his wife because he saw the choices he had made to bring his family to this, and he regretted every one of them.

"I ran into Ms. Horendeck at Safeway." Tim covered the leftovers in the stainless steel lasagna pan.

Julie crossed her arms, her lips thinned, and she began bouncing in expectation of the coming fight.

Tim saw that. He knew from experience that he could not reach his daughter through confrontation, but the same fragility that kept him from bringing the subject up at dinner now worked against him in the form of inertia.

"She asked if you were okay." He just kept going. "She thought maybe you were sick."

"That class is kind of boring." Not only was it boring, but Ms. Horendeck was a bitch. She kept Julie after class to tell her that if she stayed with her boyfriend she'd regret it.

"Ms. Horendeck said you've missed a lot of class."

"Why do you got to monitor me?" Julie backed away as she said it.

Tim was losing her. He couldn't afford that. He tried to think of something to say, something that would compel her to stay. "I'm not monitoring you."

"Bullshit!"

"Julie, please don't swear at me."

"Fuck you!"

*   *   *

Tim was at Safeway at four o'clock, when he should have been at work. He hadn't been to the office yet this week. He had no idea what he did with his time. Television mostly. That and sleep. He had a cart full of Doritos, cheese puffs, Twinkies, five gallons of ice cream, and a half dozen frozen pizzas when he ran into Ms. Horendeck near the checkout.

The only explanation for the look of shock on the woman's face he could come up with was the contents of his shopping cart. In that moment, Tim had a revelation: he would cook and invite Julie over for dinner.

As he pushed his cart, for the second time, through the aisles he felt hope. He had a plan. He would make lasagna. It was Julie's favorite dish. He would make lasagna and the two of them would sit down together at the dinner table and eat a meal, an event that had not taken place in his home since Teri left.

He loaded the ground beef, pork sausage, lasagna noodles, cans of tomato sauce and five different types of cheese in the gaps between the ice cream, frozen pizzas, and bags of chips. Tim piled the groceries onto the conveyor belt, and the pizzas were bagged by the time he realized that not only had he forgotten his wallet, but he had forgotten his pants. He was barefoot and wearing Teri's silk pajamas.

He followed Julie to her bedroom. "Your teacher found me at Safeway. She asked if you were sick. How am I monitoring you?"

"I'm too old for you to control me."

There had to be a way to reach her. He had never felt so desperate about anything. "I don't want to control you."

"Then leave me alone."

His head fell. "Okay." He stepped out of her bedroom, put his hand on the wall and looked back. There were tears welling in Julie's eyes. Whatever was happening inside her heart, it was beyond his comprehension. He knew that, but he was her father, and he wanted to comfort her. He wanted her to know that he loved her. He turned to face her, tears in his own eyes, and opened his arms.

"Don't touch me!"

* * *

Tim finished the dishes alone, then sat down on the sofa and picked up the remote. He pointed it at the TV for a minute or more, but never turned it on. He dropped the remote on the sofa and went into the kitchen. He found the Vicodin and a wine glass, but the bottle on the counter was empty. There was a syrah from Colorado Cellars, a local winery, he had been waiting to try. He headed downstairs to find it. Then the lightbulb at the bottom of the staircase blew out when he switched it on.

Tim remembered what he was like in high school. His parents were saints. He understood that now. He would call his dad in the morning and would make sure he said it. You're a saint. How did you do it? He'd ask. Because I don't know what the hell I'm doing.

He tried to comfort himself with the knowledge that Julie would grow out of it, just as he did. In some ways, she was more mature than he ever was. Julie was interested in theater. She painted and read books. Had ambition. He couldn't remember caring about anything but girls, beer, and drugs, in that order. Tim wasn't half as smart as his daughter. He knew that. Julie was gifted. If she could just get through high school, she'd be okay.

He flipped on the light in the basement storage room, found the lightbulbs on the shelf and nearly stepped on a brass cymbal someone had left on the floor. He picked it up and saw the Pearl bass drum behind a stack of boxes.

Tim's high school band stayed together until he was twenty-three, the year after they all graduated from college. By the time they broke up, they had toured both coasts, they had a record deal, and twice he had heard one of their songs on the radio.

Tim found the snare next, followed by another cymbal. He carried the bass drum out of the storage room, but he couldn't get to any more of the drum kit without moving boxes so he ferried the boxes out of the room, too. He was shirtless and sweating by the time he found the remaining pieces of his kit: mid tones, high tom, low tom, high hat, sticks, stands, and pedals. He brought it all out.

Tim was out of breath and thirsty after he carried all the boxes back into the storage room, but he didn't want to be upstairs. That's when he remembered why he had come down in the first place. He found a pair of headphones on the Sony keyboard next to the wine rack.

He plucked the cork and took a long pull from the bottle. Then he stood the coffee table on end against the wall and set up the drum kit between the couches and the TV.

It had been twenty-five years since he played. He started with the triple stroke roll warmup he learned in elementary school. Then he kicked the bass drum a few times. Tim took the phone out of his pocket and found Neil Young's "Helpless," the first song he learned. He plugged in the headphones and turned up the volume.

After Neil Young, he played "Lithium" by Nirvana, "Hot for Teacher" by Van Halen, and "Moby Dick" by Led Zeppelin.

Julie came down the stairs to ask what the fuck was going on during "My Generation" by The Who, but she forgot the question she had rehearsed during her descent when she saw her father at the drum set singing along with the chorus, "This is my generation. This is my generation, baby." By then, he had been at it for a while. His hair was drenched with sweat and flattened along his skull, his face was dripping, and his bare chest was glistening.

Tim made eye contact with her and smiled. Then, without breaking rhythm, he took a long pull from the bottle.

"Are you serious!" Julie ran upstairs and slammed the garage door as she went out of the house.

*　　*　　*

Tim hadn't seen Julie in two weeks. She was engaged to her boyfriend now. That's what Ben, his son, said, anyway. Ben stayed the night, which was nice. They grilled burgers and watched *Star Trek: Into Darkness* on Netflix. Apart from his son, Tim hadn't talked to another human being in days. His meeting with Teri was scheduled for Friday. He couldn't remember dreading anything as much as he dreaded the approach of that day. The meeting was to take place at a coffee shop near his office. Teri must've thought he was still going to work and was trying to be supportive. Tim didn't want to, but he was going to sign the divorce papers. There was nothing to gain by making it hard.

*   *   *

He opened the garage door, stepped into the house, and knew by the smell that she had been smoking. My god, he thought, at least she's home. He found Julie sitting on her bed.

"Hi, Dad." She didn't even try to hide the pipe.

Something happened in that moment that had never happened before. Tim could see all the different paths he could take. They were laid out, as if on a map, in his mind. Which is how he knew each decision he might make led to the same ever-widening chasm between himself and his daughter. It would be easy to get angry at her, but he didn't want to. He could say something about the smell, the pipe laying in plain view on her pillow, her boyfriend . . . but he rejected each of those choices in turn. He thought about mentioning how worried he was, but even that could be misconstrued as criticism. In the end, Tim settled on a single word. "Hi."

She had run away from home. She was back now and smoking marijuana in the house. The significance of those details was that they were indicators of a trauma. That she needed him.

"Hard night?" he asked.

"Yeah."

His daughter was suffering. Nothing else mattered. "Can I sit down?"

His compassion broke her. She couldn't speak and nodded her head.

He was worried for Julie and knew that he couldn't push it. If he triggered her, he'd lose this moment and with it, possibly, his daughter. He sat on the edge of the bed and left several feet between them.

Julie lit the pipe and took a hit.

Tim knew the act for what it was and held his hand out in a gesture of supplication.

The gesture puzzled Julie. She had wanted him to challenge her, to drive a wall of conflict between them, only because it was familiar. When she finally realized that he wanted to chief with her, she thought, *this ought to be interesting*, and passed the pipe.

Tim took a hit. What he didn't know was how much more potent the legal product of his daughter's generation was. But the bowl came around again and within a few minutes he was learning. Tim kicked his shoes off, got all the way onto the bed and sat with his back against the wall. Everything started slowing down, and his ability to discern in advance the destination each of his choices would bring him to intensified. What he saw in the conversation he hoped to have was a mine field, and he knew it with certainty now, if he said anything, anything at all, the situation would explode.

The long silence felt awkward to Julie, and she turned on her music player. The first song was Bob Dylan's "Tryin' to Get to Heaven."

The song's five minutes and twenty-two seconds felt like an hour to Tim. The way he understood the song was that he had broken his daughter's heart. Every verse was more painful than the last. That her suffering was his fault. He knew it. He closed his eyes and listened.

Julie sang along with the last verse, and he wanted to tell her that everything was not as hollow as it seemed. With the impulse to speak, to console her, came the simultaneous revelation of its consequence, and he held his tongue.

Tim recognized the next song as also from the album *Time Out of Mind*. This was it, he thought. He placed his hope in the music. There was a message here, a way he and Julie could communicate, but he could no longer concentrate, and regardless of his effort to do so, the song slipped from his awareness. He didn't know how much time had passed when he heard it again. It could have been seconds. Then again, it might have been minutes. By now, it might be a different song altogether, which would mean he had missed her message. How long was the average song? The problem that question posed seemed paramount, but before he could answer it, he heard the lyrics of another verse. He labored to understand what it was that Julie was trying to say to him. This was the most important thing of all, he reminded himself, listen. But his thoughts were pulsating. The rhythm of his mind seemed to accelerate. He couldn't keep up with the pulsations, and the thought was gone.

It was like death, it occurred to Tim, he was afraid of death. The rhythm of his mind began to slow down and he realized why he couldn't love Julie. The joy she brought him, her preciousness, made him afraid. He tried to enter that fear as the rhythm of his mind accelerated again. But it became too intense, the waves too close to penetrate. If he could enter it, stare it down, then he could grab her and pull both of them out.

Julie wasn't as disoriented by the marijuana as her father. She realized now that it was probably a mistake to let him have a third chase. Julie used his credit card and ordered Cosmo's.

Tim knew that she had asked for something, but he couldn't find it: the words she used. He couldn't find them. He didn't hear the doorbell ring or know that Julie had answered it. Nor did he realize how hungry he was until she offered him the pizza. Nothing else mattered, not while he ate the pizza.

The playlist seemed to have a good effect on her dad, so Julie played it again.

The rhythm of his mind was steadier now. The pulsations more stable. The wavelengths, that's what it was, they were more spread out. When he heard "Make You Feel My Love," he wanted to sing out loud. "There's nothing that I would not do, Go to the ends of the Earth for you, To make you feel my love." He thought he might be singing, but he checked and he wasn't. That would have been a mistake. The main thing, he reminded himself, was to listen. When he remembered that Julie was next to him, he also saw that she was crying. How did that happen? He wanted to comfort her.

"I was really scared when I saw you on the floor," she said.

He was lying in a pool of his own blood at the time, his head split open. Julie found her mom near death in the blood-soaked bed.

Tim reached for her hand, and she gave it to him. He was crying, too.

It no longer felt weird to be stoned with her dad, and that in itself was a little weird. Middle school was a two-year horror that began roughly around the time of her first period and ended sometime in ninth grade. The alienation she felt then she blamed on puberty and the meanness that constituted the social norms of that age.

"I was really, really scared."

That Tim could actually hear his daughter surprised him. She was speaking, and the main thing to do was listen.

By the time Julie was ready to reach out to her parents again, they were both in the hospital.

"When the paramedics put you in the ambulance, I thought I'd never see you again. It's crazy, I know, but one of the things I kept thinking about was that I'd never get to tell you where I wanted to go to college. I just wanted to get in the ambulance with you so I could tell you that. I was only fifteen years old and didn't know myself, but it was all I could think about when they took you away."

They sat on the bed holding hands, listening to Bob Dylan. In the three years since the break-in happened, no one in the family had spoken about the attack, not in any meaningful way.

"After they took you away in that ambulance, you never really came back." Julie felt her dad squeeze her hand. She looked at him and saw that he hadn't cleaned the tears from his face. "You were here, but you weren't really here."

Tim didn't know how many songs had played since Julie said that he wasn't really here. He just knew it was true. He could see her heart, and he knew it was true. Teri had nearly died in the assault. Tim felt so much shame over his inability to protect his wife, he never really came back. He had never admitted that before. But Julie was right. He also knew that he had caught up to her: their minds were now pulsating at the same frequency.

"I feel trapped. Even though I know it's me and not you, you're the only one I can fight."

In the space between her words, Tim could read things in his daughter's heart she didn't yet know about herself. All that turmoil and there was never a safe place for her to return to. What she needed was an anchor. A love she could hold on to and know was solid. That would give her the strength she needed to believe in herself.

Julie told him that she stopped going to school. She told him about the Depo-Provera shot. She told him that her boyfriend had kicked her out. Then she told him about the time in third grade she crashed her bike into his new Saab. It was the day after he bought it. The handlebar scratched the passenger door, and she was afraid that if he found out, he wouldn't love her anymore.

"I'm becoming mom, but I want to be me."

The wavelengths were far apart now, and they were coming down when she spoke again.

"I don't like myself."

He held her in his arms, and she kept repeating that.

*   *   *

The dog loped, tail thumping, out of the open garage to greet Julie when she came home from school on Thursday. Tim was in the garage with Julie's acrylic paint and brushes. He was wearing Teri's cotton bathrobe without a shirt and her silk pajamas, which on him looked like knickers.

"Dad, what are you doing?"

His answer was matter of fact: "Painting."

Tim was, in fact, painting the hood of his Saab 9-3. Her father's behavior had been so bizarre for months that anything routine might have alarmed her.

It had been Julie's first day back at school, and it wasn't an easy day. The only class she was still passing was theater, and that was with a D-.

The first thing that happened when Julie saw the pink letters painted on the black hood of her dad's car was that her jaw opened. It took her awhile to get around to actually reading the statement: "I love my daughter." As the import of her dad's act registered, the shock was converted into a smile, then that smile into laughter. Tim was holding the brush in one hand and a cup of acrylic paint in the other when Julie's laughter burst into a hug.

"Dad, are you high?"

"A little bit. Come 'ere." Tim led her to the passenger side of the car and pointed to a long, shallow scratch, barely noticeable, on the front door. "Is this the scratch?"

"I think so."

It was handlebar height and the only scratch on that side of the car.

Tim painted a pink box around it. "You know why I want to remember this scratch?"

"Why?" Julie was still laughing.

"Because it reminds me of how much I love you."

Julie decided right there in the garage that she wasn't going out of state for college. She had over a month to get her grades up. Then she would apply to CU-Boulder.

"What are you doing right now?" Tim walked around to the driver's door and got in the car. "Let's get ice cream."

Julie got in the car, and they just sat there.

Tim held the steering wheel with both hands, waiting for something to happen. "Where are my keys?"

"Oh my god, you're so stoned."

She drove them to Little Man Ice Cream on 16th Street. Tim was still in Teri's bathrobe and wasn't wearing shoes, which was okay because it was a walk-up ice cream parlor in a building designed as an old-fashioned milk can.

"Before we order," he told the cashier, "I want to show you something."

The cashier might have been seventeen, and it was clear to Julie that she didn't know what to make of her dad.

"Come on," he said and beckoned her to come outside.

The cashier looked at the line of customers behind Tim on the patio. She had a choice to make: she could cave and just deal with the loony request, or she could tough it out and try to make him go away. She took another look at Tim, who was retying the knot on his bathrobe, and realized there was no chance he would go away.

"It'll be okay," Julie assured her.

Tim's hair hadn't been combed or cut for some time. It looked like waves in a tempest. He turned to the people behind him and said, "Come on, I want to show all of you." He walked over to the fence that marked the perimeter of the patio. "Come on!"

The freshly painted Saab was parked at the curb. He was standing beside the front passenger door and waved the cashier through the crowd. They were all staring at the car.

"You see that scratch?"

The cashier looked at Julie then at the crowd behind her before she answered. "Yeah."

"My daughter put that there with her handlebars when she was in the third grade. And you know what?"

As the seconds passed, it became evident to the cashier that this wasn't going to end until she replied. "What?"

"I love my daughter."

PATRICIA FROLANDER

Bequest

During the Depression, Grandma was grateful to cook for loggers three
     times a day,
grateful to feed her son and daughter, grateful for a place to lay her head.
She chopped and hauled wood until her arms could hold no more,
then stoked the fire,
stood pigeon-toed before the Home Comfort as she fried bacon, flapjacks, eggs.
Come noon, thick gravy, boiled potatoes, fried chicken, and corn filled
     hungry bellies.

On humid afternoons she canned beans, tomatoes, peas, or pickles,
beads of perspiration on her lip and brow.
That stove never seemed to cool before another meal began.
Grandma's spoon, worn down on one side,
stirred applesauce to "just right" as her daughter played on the plank floor.
The baby cooed as Gran shucked corn and boiled beans.

Worn dollar bills were tucked each month into an old sock.
Her spoon kept stirring and her children kept growing.
Winter followed winter and each spring hungry men smiled
as chicken-fried steak joined thick slices of warm bread and churned butter.
And each spring clothes were patched
and new shoes lightened the sock.

Today the Home Comfort is stored in my shed.
Grandma and her children rest in a sunny hillside cemetery.
On my electric stove, I stir the applesauce to "just right" with the spoon
worn down on one side—
grin when I realize I stand pigeon-toed as I ladle the sauce into jars
to store on Grandma's cellar shelves.

LYLA D. HAMILTON

Bum Lambs

Perhaps my mother thought the story amusing.
     When I was young, she often told the tale:
     Twenty-six bum lambs.
     Some orphaned.
     Others rejected by their mothers.

     My mother gave them names,
     A to Z,
     From Greek myths.

     In the spring
     Of her twelfth year
     She finger-fed them cow's milk
     Until they could eat grass.
     She trained them to leap into her arms on command.

     In the summer, they fattened in the mountain meadows.
     In the fall, they went to slaughter.

          My mother spared me
          The end of the story
          Perhaps waiting until
          She deemed me
          "Old enough to understand."

               I pray
               I never
               Grow that old.

My mother may have thought the story showed
     That her taciturn father, a rancher,
     Was open-minded.
     After all,
     He took in sheep,
     An abomination to cattlemen.

Thrift
>Not tolerance
>Moved him.

That spring,
>His cattle produced too much milk.
>He didn't want to waste it.
>Couldn't afford to waste it.

The family dog
>Unnamed.
>One winter
>When icy water backed up to the ranch house
>Family and hired hands
>Rallied to save the cattle;
>Moved them to higher ground.

>"We saw the dog swimming," my mother told me.
>"That was the last anyone saw of him."
>She spoke with no apparent regret.
>No sign of pain or loss.

Her own black filly, Elaine,
>My mother named
>For the legendary woman
>Whose love of Lancelot
>Was unrequited.

My mother earned Elaine
>By getting good grades.

Later, they realized
>Cowboys had ruined Elaine for riding
>Had dragged her to break her.

My mother never uttered
A word of criticism
Or grief.
Anger
Or disappointment.

In my mother's childhood world, animals were livestock.
Valued by the pound.
Money in the bank.
Money for food
Clothing
Shelter.

My mother's sister Delia
Whose name is nearly
An anagram of mine
Suffered their father's wrath.
Banished at seventeen
Pregnant and unmarried.

The curse passed to Delia's daughter
Defiantly named
Gloria Joy.

It endured
Even after Delia's suicide
At twenty-one.

He was deliberately absent
When she was buried
In an unmarked grave
Far from home.

Gloria Joy,
Known but unacknowledged
By her mother's family,
Left to her fate,
Languished
In an orphanage.

I inhabit a world unlike my mother's.
As a curly-haired toddler
I joyously reached out
To embrace a small black dog.
Kin to me
As much as any of my siblings.

Horses, too.
Beginning with Tony,
The Palomino gelding,
A gift from my father's father.
Beloved, gentle Tony.
I thought him a member of the family.

I tried in vain
To comprehend
How my parents
Could deliberately
Leave him behind
When we moved from the ranch.

Not being of my world,
My mother couldn't imagine
The stories I heard her tell.

Ewes reject lambs.
Parents reject children.

They're not loved for who they are.
They're not unique.

They're tolerated
As long as they don't ask too much.
As long as they don't cause trouble.

Be careful not to offend
Lest you be abandoned,
Cast out.
Left to die.
Or sent to slaughter.

DON KUNZ

Lost in the Wasatch

Struggling to find our way
We discover thin traces
Worn into wildflower meadows,
Game trails stalked by ghosts.

We cross clearings where
Ancient dancers caressed
The ground that held them
In its stubborn wrinkled hand,

Follow crystal fluted notes
Singing the language of water,
Our feet feeling thunder's drum

Crackling across barren peaks.

Lost in the Wasatch
Drawn by our elders
We find a deep map;
Learn how to read.

ELLARAINE LOCKIE

Dignity's Dirty Little Secret

A German immigrant grandfather
widowed at ninety-one
Like a joint custody child
shuffled between his sons' homesteads
Two-room shacks with attics
to shelter full families
The only forms of birth control
dispensed by diphtheria and food poisoning

Fathers who broke prairie by cutting furrow
with cast iron plows
Made the families' shoes from cowhide
And tamed progeny with the same
razor strop precision
practiced by their own fathers

Mothers with gardens and perennial babies
Burdened by churned butter
and washboarded clothes
Canned a winter's worth of provisions
And divided hogs into soap
sausage and pickled pigs' feet

Children who began to baby-sit at four
Who gathered eggs, milked cows
and learned to cook and sew
Who walked three miles
to a one-room school house

No time or place for a grandfather
whose Low German dialect engendered
waves of high hate during the war
Whose spit dribbled into his white beard

And whose pee soaked the girls' straw-filled cot
while they slept on the floor

He could no longer compensate
with Grimms' fairytales
Or wrap his claw fingers around udders
But he could still tie a slipknot in a rope
And throw it over a barn rafter
Where they found him hanging
one Sunday after returning from church
The milking stool turned over beneath him

ELLARAINE LOCKIE

In the Language of Dark

—The epitaph: *Apr 1, 1935–Dec 24, 2002*
Little Walt from Big Sandy, Montana

Here in the country you ran with wild mustang energy
from the world's brightest light bulb
until the curvature of the earth switched it off
Your battery charged until the next sunrise
You fluffed up and strutted like a yard guard goose
But it's the prairie nights that told you who you were

That spoke in deep dark, foreign to a city
Where street lights and neon signs
burn bright under blankets of clouds and smog
An orange glaze suggesting dystopian fiction
Muted to the truth of an unlit night's glory
of naked stars, planets, and galaxies
The power of a silver-tongued moon

Its command of the ocean's tide
and of your internal clockwork
That essential day and night rhythm compromised
So you would come to the country where dark
isn't silenced by reflection or refraction
Where it underwrites in unmatched volume
a brilliance of height and breadth
which became your measuring stick

And now you're the one who reflects
your sixty-seven years
The one who defies gravity
when deepest dark whispers a grave-top oratory
in your own words from under
the soundproofing of dense prairie soil

VICTORIA WADDLE

Marathon Fire

The midnight blast of sirens startled me awake. Blaring up and down our street, the voice of a bullhorn, with its automated urgency, commanded, "You must evacuate." When I had fallen asleep, two cities and a horizon full of rolling hills had separated my Claremont, California neighborhood from the Grand Prix fire. Everything had changed in a few hours, as a hot October Santa Ana swept the fire west.

I rose, stupid with sleep, my torso and limbs aching from that morning's seventeen-mile jog. In six weeks, I was due to run the Honolulu Marathon with the Leukemia Society's Team in Training. Early that day I'd been buoyant, running better than in two previous years of training, with a realistic hope of cutting at least fifteen minutes from my personal record. My fundraising was going well; my honoree was beating her cancer.

I rubbed a cramp from my right hamstring and hitch-stepped toward the front door while I shook loose thoughts of the marathon. My husband, even more sleep-addled than I, told me he was going to take a shower before we left. I looked out into the night to see whether I could glimpse the fire now that it was moving in our direction. A fifty-foot wall of flame covered the adjacent hills as far as I could see to the east. Even then, it must have been a few miles away, but it enveloped my senses, the scorch and ash in my nose, the heat pulling my skin as though I had stepped into a dehydrator, the infernal crackling dance of the orange-red curtain causing me to squint.

I ran back into my bedroom to find my husband picking out clothes. "Now, now!" I said, and pointed. He, too, went to have a look.

My God, I thought. *What am I supposed to take?* I walked down our long hallway, knowing that a smart woman would grab the portraits off the wall. But I couldn't think beyond my family and the dog.

I awakened my three sons, my thoughts slow. Their pajamas, with designs of dinosaurs, planets, and electric guitars, were indicative of their ages—six, nine, and thirteen. Considering that span, they might have had varying reactions to the midnight awakening and the encircling fire. Yet each of them exuded a calm wonder, an awe of nature that was removed from panic. They stood in the doorway, barefoot. God knows where their slippers were, they never wore them, and there was no time to look now. "Go grab your tennis shoes. And shut the door. You're letting smoke in," I said.

We leashed our husky-mix of a mutt, who was excited about a ride in the car on any terms, and piled into the minivan. Our street itself appeared menacing, lit eastward in blood and ginger orange, but pitch behind us. The blaze, with its swirling cinders, had the same broiler effect on us as we faced it, the heat choking us without surrounding us. We fled.

After dropping our children off at my in-laws' home in the adjacent city, my husband and I drove as near as we were allowed to our neighborhood, about three-quarters of a mile away. It was a masochistic thing to do. The area was now on fire, and from this distance it was impossible to see which homes had gone up in flames. There was no fire brigade, the blaze having spread much farther than the local fire departments were able to reach.

We couldn't stay—not for the grief of it, but because a weird weather system had enveloped us with fierce swirling winds, carrying ash hot enough to burn. The smoke seared our eyes and marred our vision. The campfire smell that all of my life had signaled pleasure had now intensified to a choking stink. There was that same sense of baking that I had experienced earlier.

We turned away. Lines from an antique poem rose from a memory I didn't know existed. Several years earlier, I had read "Upon the Burning of Our House, July 10, 1666" by the Puritan poet Anne Bradstreet. Those few words that I recalled were both a sound in my mind and a vision across the screen of fire.

> And, when I could no longer look,
> I blest his Name that gave and took . . .
>
> Farewell my pelf, farewell my store.
> The world no longer let me love,
> My hope and treasure lies above.

With no fire trucks in sight, I was trying to let go, to release hope, and with it, all my material possessions. It didn't work. I wanted the fire department, and I wanted my home, the tiny things that, gathered together, reminded me of who I was.

Back at my in-laws', I tried to close my eyes, but each time I did, a wall of flame appeared inside my eyelids. I wondered if I was hallucinating. A list of what I should have taken from the house—beginning with my computer—started a spinning cycle through my head.

Just after we quit our vigil, the fire crews arrived from hundreds of miles away in Northern California, coming in on the only open street and facing down flames in three directions.

Along with our neighbors, we had the opportunity to thank the fire crews the following afternoon. Packed tightly in the local high school gym, the crowd clapped as the city fire chief was introduced. "You'll be allowed back into the area tonight. Some of you are not going to like what you see," he reminded us. "But, the important thing is that no one lost their life." As he detailed what was known of the damage, a contingent at the south end of the gym became agitated. Their neighborhood of over fifty houses had burned to the ground, except one. The fire crews hadn't attempted to save it because the street into the sector was too narrow for a fire truck to turn around in. This was a known hazard and houses there were uninsurable. The owners had gambled and lost everything. Now they needed someone to blame.

The vitriolic shouting blanketed my survivor's euphoria, snuffing it out. My husband and I left to buy a flashlight, so that we could assess the damage to our home through darkness, as soon as we were allowed to return.

That night, we drove slowly, disturbing haunted ground. Under the shadowy street lamps, it appeared that the Almighty had played a game of "Duck, Duck, Goose" in my immediate area, arbitrarily tapping a sprinkling of homes for destruction. The street below mine had many charcoal patches where houses stood two days before. The houses on my short street stood, though some were roofless, open to the sky. My own home was whole.

After tripping over lawn furniture that must have been thrown hastily aside by firemen as they entered the yard to do battle, I shone the flashlight in the center of a pile of ash that had been my dog's house. My knees buckled with my first real sense of proximity to loss. I pointed the flashlight up to the burnt pine tree that had dropped embers not only on the doghouse, but on all the surrounding bushes as well, igniting even the succulents growing along the wall of my home—which survived simply because the roof was gravel and rock, and the large wooden eaves were entirely covered in plaster.

Dumb luck, I thought, sympathetic to those neighbors who were now homeless. Armed with a guilt-stained gratitude, I vowed that if people could face cancer, surely I could face the remainder of my training in the charred conditions of this new proving ground. My job was to get over it and get moving.

An intellectual understanding of this was simple enough; emotionally, I faltered. The immediate area was filled with fire crews monitoring hot spots that dotted the remaining tinder. So small that they shouldn't have appeared threatening, these mini flames rattled my spine. I couldn't douse the images of fire spouts from the underworld. My midnight evacuation had altered my sense of home. I had become afraid of danger that had passed.

Taking "you are what you pretend to be" as my motto, I overlaid my dread with a mask of self-assurance. As demolition crews and landscapers worked the surrounding streets, I dug and planted in my yard, tossed out the patio furniture, its mesh seating melted by falling cinders. I grieved to have my lanky pine cut down, now certain that the fire had killed it.

Through the weeks of falling snowflake ash, I jogged slowly, wondering what I was breathing in, stopping regularly to blink the soot from my eyes. I surveyed the bare brown hills, which from a distance had a gentle, rolling sensuousness. But nearer, the physical flaws appeared. The stubs of burned Manzanita and the prickly black twig remnants of other chaparral now appeared as bristles bursting through the backs of monstrous beasts. I came upon the remains of what had been a giant cactus patch, its blackness slick, almost oily. A few pale yellow paddles poked out in each direction, a compass to orient me in the center of universal destruction.

By November, I had stopped jogging and only attempted to walk—at night, through darkness, where the fire damage was indiscernible, except in the beam of my flashlight. I could only manage a few inches of the devastation at once.

A week into December, my training schedule expired. I reunited with my teammates at the airport and traveled to Honolulu to run. Long hours into the flight, I peered out the airplane window, thinking *green* and *blue*, not as adjectives to describe the lush vegetation and deep ocean of Hawaii, but as nouns, alien things, forgotten in the blistered landscape of my home.

Despite the beauty of the racecourse, and although I didn't hit the proverbial "runner's wall," I was weary of being in the race by the halfway point. By the time I had reached the twenty-mile marker, other marathoners began to pull up beside me and ask, "Are you all right?"

"Oh, yes!" I answered with false cheer, thinking it a strange question. I was certainly moving slowly, but so were they—or they wouldn't have been in my vicinity. Why would any of them worry about me?

When I looked up to see professional photographers and a finish line banner, I pulled myself into an attitude of victory. The photographers, however, missed my finish and the pose was lost. Instead they caught a candid image, just before I thought to pose. It showed a woman with her back slumped, shoulders curved in, and her leg and foot pulled up rather than out ahead. I looked a lot more like I was trying to curl into the fetal position than make forward progress. Now I knew why fellow runners had shown concern. This was no victory. My finish was just another lap in a longer course.

Home again, I noted that the charring on the walls of my house appeared to be permanent shadows of the Grand Prix's flames. I climbed the dusty path into the hills behind my neighborhood, taking in the panoramic view of the meadow. The landscape remained scorched, covered in black grasshoppers. Nothing that was important to me—marathon training, advancements in cancer research, a life fully lived—would ever again appear to progress in a straight line from start to finish. I had come to respect the cycle, the rhythm of the environment in which I lived. I vowed to once more participate in that cycle.

Finally, come May, I stepped into a pasture of stunted blonde grass to see eucalyptus trees, their slim trunks, stark black for months, now covered in foliage—leaves were sprouting directly out of the entire surface of trees, from base to slender tip, living fire, green flames snapping, dancing out on the few remaining limbs.

I had a new image for the burning bush that was not consumed, for what it means to stand on sacred ground.

STEVEN WINGATE

Octet in Praise of Colorado's Viscera

Beloved Colorado, while I lived as a parasite in your viscera I was nothing
at all like a Colorado person. Barely hiked, couldn't afford to ski. A total
flatlander, desiccating on the plains. I could have blown away from you,
like a speck in that *Dust in the Wind* song I publicly reviled back in the
seventies but secretly sang to myself when walking alone among your
brittle grasses and embracing your emptiness. That was the beginning
of my vast desire for space, and I owe it all to you. Not to your famous
mountains but to your plains, which reached their palms toward the
rest of the world and made me simultaneously grateful for a home and
curious for my eventual escape from it.

Beloved Colorado, while I lived as a parasite in your viscera I participated
in a twentieth century version of manifest destiny: the relentless
Westward Ho of the rootless and desperate, the disgorged descendants
of those who had once been expelled from the cloaca of Ellis Island into
the swamps and pustules of New Jersey. We manifested our destiny by
getting the hell out of there and throwing ourselves at your feet, begging
for your blessing. We held our heads and hearts high but our tails hung
down between our legs, shaking as we secretly wished that no one from
back home would ever find us again. Secretly wished that you would
transforms us, by your succor, into whatever you needed us to be.

Beloved Colorado, while I lived as a parasite in your viscera I dreamed
about New Jersey all the time, though I thought I was dreaming of
New York. I compared you to my ancestral home, to my Old Country,
and found you so lacking in hot dog carts and pretzel carts and cheap
ethnic foods of questionable provenance that I abhorred you for your
simplicity and railed against you as a backwater. Found you so lacking
in these comforts that I moved away from you half a dozen times in
search of the cosmopolitan.

Beloved Colorado, while I lived as a parasite in your viscera I had no idea that you would become as cosmopolitan as you are today, with your head shops and oxygen bars and topiary gardens and smart-drug boutiques. Had I known this earlier, would I have been wise enough to stay nestled where I was, in the soft tissue just above the vestige of your appendix? Might I have saved myself trouble and money by simply waiting it out and letting nature take its course, over-populating you to the point where you became interesting? To the point where the angst and pretzel carts I loved from the Old Country lined your sidewalks like quicksand?

Beloved Colorado, while I lived as a parasite in your viscera it never occurred to me that I was actually your disease: one of many waves of internal immigrants who came to fill in a space that we labeled *empty*. Immigrants from the armpit of New York, followed later by immigrants from the armpits of Texas and California and Seattle. Which armpit will be next, beloved? And to which armpit will you send those who now live inside of *your* armpits, which fester with overpopulation at last? Perhaps South Dakota, where I live now, which is as empty as Colorado was back in the seventies. Send my fellow rejects here! Tell them there's a better place where they can find plentiful meaningless jobs and exponentially greater opportunities to fuck up without anyone they know watching.

Beloved Colorado, while I lived as a parasite in your viscera I enjoyed my rightful share of the marijuana you are now famous for. I indulged myself in that veil of haze until my ego and alter-ego became facing mirrors and I reflected infinitely on myself (while somehow remaining forever lost to myself). My divided mind couldn't decide whether to reclaim that patch of skin near the vestige of your appendix, or leave you in search of better ethnic street food once more. In the midst of my stoner indecision you rocked me on your bosom, nursing me back into something like free will, and I repaid you by scorning you once again. Will you ever forgive me for my betrayals?

Beloved Colorado, while I lived as a parasite in your viscera your mountains— your distant mountains I could never afford—made me feel impossibly insignificant, and I felt ashamed of myself. For I was too trapped in my dual-mirrored mind to understand the beauty of insignificance, or to even appreciate its intricacies on a purely intellectual level. But now I have come to love that feeling of insignificance. Sign me up, please! Give me a new home beneath your skin that allows me *absolute* insignificance! Perhaps this is what I've always wanted. Perhaps this is why I keep coming back to you like an addict.

Beloved Colorado, while I lived as a parasite in your viscera I once cried at the sight of a housing development, its peaked roofs emerging from the red earth like the vertebrae of a gargantuan dinosaur. I saw the line of roofs extending as far as I could see through what had once been fields of corn, and I wept for you, my beloved! Pulled over to the side of the highway and wept! Mourned the fact that you can never again offer another soul the emptiness you offered me. Oh my beloved! I wish—even pray, though it is out of fashion these days—that you will grant me one last share of your emptiness before it whisks itself away from you forever.

CONTRIBUTOR NOTES

Contributor Notes

Rebecca Aronson lives in New Mexico, where she teaches writing, facilitates a community writing group, and coordinates a visiting writer's series at Central New Mexico Community College. Her first book, *Creature, Creature,* was published in 2007. She has poems recently in *Quarterly West, MARY, Pilgrimage, The Paris American,* and others. She was the winner of a Prairie Schooner Strousse Award, The Loft's Speakeasy Prize, and has been the recipient of several Pushcart nominations. She is a member of the literary collective Dirt City Writers.

Betsy Bernfeld is a librarian and lawyer in Jackson Hole, Wyoming. She is a recipient of the Frank Nelson Doubleday Award for a Woman Writer, and two of her short plays have been produced by Jackson's Riot Act, Inc. Her anthology of historical Wyoming poetry, *Sagebrush Classics: Pure Wyoming Stuph,* was published by Media Publishing in Kansas City, MO.

Heidi E. Blankenship is a native of Utah. She has been hiking ever since she could walk and writing ever since she could hold a pen. Her poetry has appeared in many publications, including the anthology *Going Down Grand: Poems from the Canyon.* She has been a ranger since 1998.

For **Kaye Lynne Booth**, writing is her passion, with published work both online and in print. With a MFA in Creative Writing, she freelances and always has at least three WIPs going. Kaye also publishes items of interest in the literary world on her blog "Writing to be Read" at KAYELYNNEBOOTH.WORDPRESS.COM.

Sarah B. Boyle is a poet, mother, activist, and high school teacher. She is the author of the chapbook *What's pink & shiny/what's dark & hard* (Porkbelly Press), and her writing has appeared in *Menacing Hedge, Eratio,* and elsewhere. She is a founding editor of the Pittsburgh Poetry Houses. Find her online at IMPOLITELINES.COM.

John Brantingham is the author of seven books of poetry and fiction including his latest, *Dual Impressions: Poetic Conversations About Art*. He is a Professor of English at Mt. San Antonio College.

William Cass has had a little over ninety short stories accepted for publication in a variety of literary magazines and anthologies such as *december, Briar Cliff Review*, and *Conium Review*. Recently, he was a finalist for *Glimmer Train's* short fiction and Black Hill Press's novella competitions, received a Pushcart Prize nomination, and won writing contests at *Terrain.org* and *The Examined Life Journal*. He lives and works as an educator in San Diego, California.

Poems by **David Lavar Coy** have appeared previously in *Manifest West*. He lives in Arizona and is a retired professor of English and creative writing. He was once a young man living in Wyoming on a homestead at Polecat Bench. He is author of two-and-a-half poetry books: *Rural News, Lean Creatures*, and *Down Time to Tombstone* (Beatlick Press 2012) with David Tammer.

Benjamin Dancer is an adviser at a Colorado high school where he has made a career out of mentoring young people as they come of age. He is the author of *Patriarch Run*, and he also writes about parenting and education. He has been featured in *Bitch* magazine, *The Humanist, Truthout, The Copperfield Review, The Denver Post*, and various other magazines and journals.

For thirty-six years, **Gail Denham's** writing and photography has appeared in numerous publications. Presently concentrated on poetry, Gail leads writing/photography workshops and belongs to a dozen state poetry societies. Married fifty-seven years, she has four sons and many grandchildren. Gail loves the challenge of new poetry forms. Muses include humor, story, family, faith, and fun. Recent credits include poetry in newsletters, a poem accepted in *Marathon*, and a win in the Arizona State Poetry Society contest.

Past Wyoming Poet Laureate **Patricia Frolander** and her husband, Robert, own his family ranch in the Black Hills of Wyoming. Patricia's first book, *Grassland Genealogy*, was published in 2009 followed by her second, *Married Into It*, which garnered the National Cowboy and Western Heritage Museum's coveted Wrangler Award for Best Poetry Book of 2011, The Willa Cather Award for Best Poetry Book by Women Writing the West, and 2012 Best Woman Writer by High Plains Book Awards.

John Haggerty is the founding editor of the *Forge Literary Magazine*. His work has appeared in many publications, including *Confrontation*, *Nimrod*, *Santa Monica Review*, and *Salon*. He has an MFA in creative writing from San Francisco State University.

Lyla D. Hamilton's writing often reflects her Western roots and her interest in the human-animal bond. She holds a PhD in philosophy from UCLA and lives in Boulder County, Colorado, with her canine companion, Luke Skywalker. Her goddaughter, Chiquita, is a strawberry roan Medicine Hat mustang from Montezuma County, Colorado.

Michael Harty's poetry has appeared in *Texas Poetry Calendar, San Pedro River Review, Concho River Review, New Letters*, and elsewhere. His chapbook, *The Statue Game*, was published in 2014. He lives and writes in the Kansas City area, where he has had a long career as a psychologist and psychoanalyst.

Rick Kempa edited the anthology *ON FOOT: Grand Canyon Backpacking Stories* (Flagstaff: Vishnu Temple Press, 2014) and co-edited, with Peter Anderson, *Going Down Grand: Poems from the Canyon* (Fruita: Lithic Press, 2015). His latest poetry collection is *Ten Thousand Voices* (Oakland: Littoral Press, 2014). He lives in Rock Springs, Wyoming. Find him at RICKKEMPA.COM.

Don Kunz taught literature and film studies at the University of Rhode Island for thirty-six years. His essays, poems, and short stories have appeared in over seventy literary journals. Don has retired to Bend, Oregon, where he is a member of the five-man, philanthropic High Desert Poetry Cell.

Ellaraine Lockie's eleventh chapbook, *Where the Meadowlark Sings*, won the 2014 Encircle Publication's Chapbook Contest. Her newest collection, *Love Me Tender in Midlife*, has been released as an internal chapbook in IDES from Silver Birch Press. Ellaraine teaches poetry workshops and serves as Poetry Editor for the lifestyles magazine *Lilipoh*.

Nathan Alling Long lives in Philadelphia and teaches creative writing and literature at Stockton University. His work appears in over a hundred publications, including *Tin House, Glimmer Train, Story Quarterly*, and *Crab Orchard Review*. He is currently seeking publication for his story collection *Everything Merges with the Night* and a collection of flash fiction, *The Fortunate*.

Sarah Fawn Montgomery holds a PhD in creative writing from the University of Nebraska-Lincoln, where she works as *Prairie Schooner*'s Nonfiction Assistant Editor. The author of *The Astronaut Checks His Watch* (Finishing Line Press), her work has appeared in *Crab Orchard Review, DIAGRAM, Fugue, North Dakota Quarterly, Pinch, Puerto del Sol, Southeast Review, Terrain,* and others.

Juan J. Morales is the author of *The Siren World* and *Friday and the Year That Followed*. He is a CantoMundo Fellow, the Editor of *Pilgrimage Magazine*, and an Associate Professor of English at Colorado State University-Pueblo, where he directs the Creative Writing Program and curates the SoCo Reading Series.

Lance Nizami has no formal training in the Arts. As of January 2016, he has 185 poems in print or in press (not online), some recent acceptances being at *Petrichor Machine* and at *Dewpoint*.

Ronald Pickett is a retired naval aviator who was born and raised in Phoenix, AZ. He writes, paints, exercises, and travels extensively. The majority of his published work has been in the field of leadership and management. He has two published books, *Perfect Crimes: I Got Away With It*, and *Discovering Roots: The Story of a Family's Return to Ethiopia, the Birthplace of Their Adopted Daughters*. Both are available on Kindle.

Terry Severhill has been writing since about 1966. He is a former combat Marine, former construction worker, and a former toddler. His work has appeared in *A Quiet Courage, Damnfino, Mad Swril, Teeny Tiny, Red Omnivore*, and *Proud to Be: Writing by American Warriors* (fourth in a series of anthologies by Southeast Missouri University Press). He is the winner of the Art Young Memorial Award for Poetry 2016 (*Garbanzo Literary Journal*) and he'll be making his fourth appearance in the anthology *The San Diego Poetry Annual*.

David Stallings was born in the American South, raised in Alaska and Colorado before settling in the Pacific Northwest. Once an academic geographer, he has long worked to promote public transportation in the Puget Sound area. His poems have appeared in several North American, U.K., and Swedish literary journals and anthologies, and in *Resurrection Bay*, a recent Evening Street Press chapbook.

Scott T. Starbuck, a co-creative writing coordinator at San Diego Mesa College, has a new book of climate change poems, *Industrial Oz: Ecopoems* (Fomite, 2015). *Lost Salmon*, his book of fishing poems/climate change poems is forthcoming (MoonPath, 2016). His poems have appeared in *Los Angeles Review, Confronation,* and *Canary*.

Abigail Van Kirk is a student at Pikes Peak Community College, and her horse Molly is her constant companion and keeps her creative. This in turn inspires her to capture cadences around her, from human nature to nature surrounding her. Abigail's work has been published by *US Represented, Spare Cat Press*, and elsewhere.

Victoria Waddle has been published in literary journals and was recently nominated for a Pushcart Prize. She is a *Bosque Magazine* Fiction Prize finalist and is included in *Best Short Stories from the Saturday Evening Post Great American Fiction Contest 2016*. She reviews books at SCHOOLLIBRARYLADY.COM and contributes to the Inland Empire's *Press Enterprise* "Literary Journeys."

Evan Morgan Williams' book of stories, *Thorn*, won the Chandra Prize at BkMk Press (University of Missouri-Kansas City). He has published over forty stories in literary magazines including *Kenyon Review, Zyzzyva, Alaska Quarterly Review*, and *Witness*. He is currently at work on a novel and a collection of stories set in the Rocky Mountain West.

Steven Wingate is a multi-genre author whose work, ranging from print to interactive, includes the prize-winning short story collection *Wifeshopping* (2008) and the digital lyric memoir *daddylabyrinth*, which premiered in 2014 at the ArtScience Museum of Singapore. He teaches at South Dakota State University.

About the Staff

Sheena Feiler is a proud Colorado native who graduated from the University of Colorado Boulder with a BA in English Literature. Motivated by her dream to become an editor, she is studying as a graduate student in the Publishing Certificate at Western State Colorado University and working as an editorial intern for Conundrum Press.

Sapphire Heien is a graduate student in Publishing at Western State Colorado University. She holds a bachelor's degree in English and Professional Writing from the University of Wyoming, and she lives in Laramie, Wyoming, with her husband and their far too many books.

Caleb J. Seeling is the Director of the Certificate in Publishing at Western State Colorado University. He began working in publishing in 2006 and founded Samizdat Publishing Group in Denver in 2009. The company has since expanded, forming two imprints (Conundrum Press and Samizdat Creative), publishing between 20-30 books altogether each year. An active member of several publishing and arts organizations, Caleb is also a social entrepreneur, finding ways to serve the greater community and disadvantaged youth through strategic partnerships.

Mark Todd is Editor-in-Chief at Western Press Books and has taught at Western State Colorado University since 1988. He's author of seven books: two collections of poetry, a science fiction novel, and co-author with wife Kym O'Connell-Todd of the paranormal comedy *Silverville Saga* trilogy, as well as a creative nonfiction book on haunted hotels.

Sonya Unrein is a freelance editor and book designer. She has a master's degree from the University of Denver in Digital Media Studies, and lives near Denver with her husband and cat.